NE • MICKEY TETTLETON • MATT NOKES • HANK

DER • TONY CLARK • CHARLIE GEHRINGER • LOU

DIE MAYO • ALAN TRAMMELL UENN •

VIS FRYMAN • GEORGE KELL • PINKY

RTON • ROCKY COLAVITO • GOOSE GOSLIN • HEINIE

MON • RON LeFLORE • HOOT EVERS • AL KALINE •

MAGGLIO ORDONEZ • HAL NEWHOUSER • MICKEY

AGUIRRE • DENNY McLAIN • JIM BUNNING • JACK

ROWE • JOHN HILLER • WILLIE HERNANDEZ • TODD

NDERSON • MAYO SMITH • STEVE O'NEILL • HUGHIE

COCHRANE • MICKEY TETTLETON • MATT NOKES •

IELDER • TONY CLARK • CHARLIE GEHRINGER • LOU

DIE MAYO • ALAN TRAMMELL • HARVEY KUENN •

VIS FRYMAN • GEORGE KELL • RAY BOONE • PINKY

RTON • ROCKY COLAVITO • GOOSE GOSLIN • HEINIE

MON • RON LeFLORE • HOOT EVERS • AL KALINE •

MAGGLIO ORDONEZ • HAL NEWHOUSER • MICKEY

AGUIRRE • DENNY McLAIN • JIM BUNNING • JACK

ROWE • JOHN HILLER • WILLIE HERNANDEZ • TODD

FEW AND CHOSEN

Defining Tigers Greatness Across the Eras

Lance Parrish

with Phil Pepe

TRIUMPH
BOOKS

Triumph Books and colophon are registered trademarks of Random House, Inc.

Library of Congress Cataloging-in-Publication Data

Parrish, Lance.
  Few and chosen : defining Tigers greatness across the eras /
Lance Parrish with Phil Pepe.
      p. cm.
  Includes index.
  ISBN 978-1-60078-286-2
  1. Detroit Tigers (Baseball team)—History. I. Pepe, Phil. II. Title.

  GV875.D6P37 2010
  796.357'640977434—dc22

                                      2009048980

This book is available in quantity at special discounts for your group or organization. For further information, contact:

> **Triumph Books**
> 542 South Dearborn Street
> Suite 750
> Chicago, Illinois 60605
> (312) 939-3330
> Fax (312) 663-3557
> www.triumphbooks.com

Printed in U.S.A.
ISBN: 978-1-60078-286-2

Design by Nick Panos; page production by Patricia Frey
All photos courtesy of Getty Images unless otherwise noted

As ballplayers, we often go through our days, our years, and our careers so focused on our jobs that we unwittingly take for granted the lives we leave behind when we go to the ballpark or embark on a two-week road trip. With that in mind, I wish to acknowledge my wife Arlyne and my children David, Matthew, and Ashley for their love and unwavering support and for enduring without complaint the sometimes trying absence of a husband and father for periods of time when a husband and father is what they needed most.

Professional athletes never can get back the time lost with loved ones, but if I may make one suggestion to today's athletes, it's this: make the most of the time you have during your career and spend as much quality time as possible with loved ones.

So, to Arlyne, David, Matthew and Ashley, for your understanding, your support, and your patience as I pursued my dream of playing the game I love, I say "Thank you." I love you all very much.

Contents

Foreword

I was there as a television announcer when Lance Parrish joined the Tigers in 1977 and when he left Detroit nine years later. In between, I had the pleasure of watching a young man develop into an outstanding major league catcher, and I acquired a friend for life.

I still remember vividly the first time I saw Lance. It was in Lakeland, Florida, in the spring of 1975. He was a kid of 18 at the time, and he had been the Tigers' No. 1 draft pick the previous June. You couldn't help notice him and be impressed with him because he had a certain look about him. He was considered a great prospect, and he looked the part: an all-American-looking guy, 6'3", with a great athletic body and a cannon for an arm.

Lance had turned down a football scholarship at UCLA to sign with the Tigers. He was the first baseball player I can remember who was really serious about lifting weights. In those days, weights were considered taboo for baseball players, but they certainly didn't hurt Lance Parrish.

Despite my initial impression of Lance as a physical specimen, I must admit that when I first saw him I never expected him to become one of the best catchers in Detroit Tigers history—which is exactly what he is. In high school, he had pitched and played just about every position on the diamond. The Tigers drafted him as an infielder and played him at third base in his first year in the minor leagues before they switched him to catcher. As soon as he began to concentrate on catching, he developed in a big way—literally!

During his years with the Tigers, Lance became affectionately known as "the Big Wheel." And he truly was that, a big deal with the Tigers. To this day, the people of Detroit still love him.

Along with Alan Trammell, Kirk Gibson, Lou Whitaker, and Jack Morris, Lance was a key player on the Tigers' 1984 World Series–winning team. He had a great career with the Tigers on the field, and he was a leader in the clubhouse as well. I can honestly say I have never heard anybody say a bad word about him.

As a member of the Tigers' television broadcasting team in those days, I got to spend a good deal of time with Lance over the years, and we became good friends. I found him to be an easy guy to like, not only a great player but also a great person. And he has a great family. My wife, Louise, and I have really enjoyed the time we have spent around Lance and his family, watching his kids grow up.

I remember how Lance agonized over his decision when he became a free agent after the 1986 season. The night he had to make his decision, Louise and I took Lance and his wife, Arlyne, and Bill Freehan and his wife, Pat, to dinner at the Oakland Hills Country Club. After dinner, we all went back to our house, and I said to him, "Lance, you know it's getting close to midnight, and you've got to make a decision."

He said, "I've already made my decision."

That's when I learned that his decision was to leave the Tigers and accept the free-agent offer from the Philadelphia Phillies.

Although I respected his decision and I understood his desire to do what he believed was best to provide for his family, as a member of the Detroit Tigers family, I couldn't help being disappointed. Lance could have owned the city of Detroit. He could have done anything he wanted to do in Detroit, careerwise and businesswise—broadcasting, television, radio…whatever he wanted—if he had stayed with the Tigers throughout his entire playing career.

That being said, it doesn't change how I feel about Lance Parrish. Or how Tigers fans feel about him. Here in Detroit, he will always be "the Big Wheel."

—Al Kaline

Preface

My journey to the major leagues actually began on my sixth birthday. Let me explain.

On that date, June 15, 1962, I was on an airplane with my mom and my sister, heading for our new home in Southern California.

My mom and dad met when they were both serving in the U.S. Marines. My dad was from Pittsburgh, and my mom was from Clairton, Pennsylvania, a small town about 20 miles southeast of Pittsburgh. When they left the marines, my mom and dad settled in Clairton, which is surrounded by towns such as Canonsburg, Donora, and McKeesport, which most sports fans will recognize as football country.

Had my dad not become weary of the hard Pennsylvania winters and decided to move to California, I probably would have grown up in that football hotbed and possibly, with any luck, gone on to play football at Penn State or the University of Pittsburgh and, if I was even luckier, gone on to play in the National Football League.

After his discharge from the marines, Dad joined the Clairton Police Department and spent several years walking a beat, both in the summer, when it was hot and humid, and in the winter, when it was nasty and snowy and freezing. The winters were the worst, and one day Dad said to Mom, "That's it. I've had it."

It happened that Mom had an older brother and some cousins living in Southern California, and they told my dad that they had heard the Los

Angeles County Sheriff's Department was expanding its police force and was looking for men to go to the academy. My dad thought this was a perfect opportunity, so he took off for California—he didn't have enough money at the time to bring the rest of the family with him—entered the Sheriff's Academy, made it through, and became a deputy sheriff in Los Angeles County. Then he sent for the rest of the family.

I played football in high school, was recruited by quite a few colleges, and signed a letter of intent to go to UCLA to play football. But growing up in Southern California, where the weather is conducive to playing baseball year-round, I was able to hone my baseball skills enough that I was taken in the first round of the June 1974 free-agent draft. I have often wondered if that would have happened if my family had stayed in Pennsylvania where the weather limited the opportunity to play baseball to just a few months a year.

By my senior year at Walnut High School, I began to attract the attention of scouts and was invited to several major league showcases. One of them was a semiprivate workout held by the Padres, who had the No.1 pick in the upcoming draft. There were only three of us: Lonnie Smith, Garry Templeton, and me. We went through all the usual stuff, hitting, throwing, and then we ended by running the 60-yard dash. It was like I was standing still; Smith and Templeton went right by me.

I also attended an Angels workout at Anaheim Stadium, where I hit quite a few balls out of the park and fielded and threw well. I thought I had made a pretty good impression. I left feeling good about myself. I figured that the Angels had to be impressed with me, and I thought I had a good chance of being drafted by them.

As I was leaving Anaheim Stadium, I was taken through the visiting clubhouse, and I noticed Detroit Tigers in the laundry bin. I figured that they were in town to play the Angels and didn't think anything of it until a few weeks later when the Tigers drafted me. I can't help but wonder if the Tigers had somebody at the workout watching me.

I was the Tigers' first choice in the June 1974 free-agent draft, the 16th pick overall. But instead of being elated, I was disappointed—I had convinced myself that the Angels would draft me, and I was bummed when they didn't take me with their 10th pick. Instead, they chose Mike Miley, a shortstop out of LSU who would play in 84 games for the Angels before he was tragically killed in an automobile accident in 1977 at age 23.

With the first pick in the draft, the Padres, who had held that exclusive workout for Lonnie Smith, Garry Templeton, and me, passed on all three of us and took shortstop Billy Almon out of Brown University. Smith was the No. 3 pick by the Phillies, and the Cardinals selected Templeton with the 13th pick. Also taken in the first round of that draft were Dale Murphy; Willie Wilson; Whitey Ford's son, Eddie; Rick Sutcliffe; and Rich Dauer.

The official release of the June 1974 draft from Major League Baseball has the Tigers selecting me as a third baseman, which has led to speculation that I was converted from the infield to catcher after I turned pro. That's one misconception I want to clear up.

I was a catcher as far back as I can remember, all the way to Little League. In my first year in Little League, it was one of those deals where the coach said, "We need a catcher. Who wants to catch?" Nobody else volunteered, so I said, "I'll do it."

I caught throughout Little League, Pony League, American Legion, and high school, but I also played other positions. I pitched, played the infield and the outfield, but catching has always been my primary position, until my senior year in high school. We had another guy who could catch, but we didn't have anybody who played third base, so my coach put me there. I had a good year with the bat, but I was surprised when the Tigers drafted me at the position.

I still wasn't sure I wanted to play baseball. The thought of playing football at UCLA was very appealing, but I figured I at least had to listen to what the Tigers had to say. Jack Deutsch, a Tigers scout, came to our house to try to get me to sign, and my dad and I sat in the living room with him. I wasn't all that determined to get the deal done on the first day. I knew I had the UCLA scholarship in my back pocket, and I was still a little hesitant about signing with the Tigers, knowing that if I signed on the dotted line I would be leaving home for who knew how long. I had never been away from home in my entire life.

I was thinking, *Do I want to do this? Or would I rather go to college right down the road, close enough that I could come home just about whenever I want to?*

It's a tough decision for an 18-year-old to have to make, but at least I was confident that whatever choice I made, the Tigers and baseball or UCLA and football, I couldn't go wrong.

The Tigers' offer was about $55,000. I told Deutsch that it was a fair and generous offer and I appreciated it, but I wasn't prepared to sign right then.

I wanted to think about it. With that, my dad jumped in and said to Jack, "Do you mind if we go into the back room to discuss this?"

"No," Jack said. "Go ahead."

My dad and I went into the back room and—I'll never forget this—my dad, who probably didn't make $55,000 in three years back then, said to me, "Do you know how much money that is?"

I said I knew it was a lot of money, but I needed to think about it. I didn't know if I wanted to do it. My dad couldn't understand my hesitation, but we went back, and I told Deutsch, "I need to think about this. I can't give you an answer right now."

And as everybody usually does in these negotiations, Jack said, "The Tigers said this is all I can give you. It's the best offer they can make."

I said, "Fine. I'm not trying to hold you up. I just need some time to think about it."

Deutsch came back the next day and bumped the Tigers' "final offer" up another $5,000 and added some incentives that, if I met them, would bring the total to $67,500. It wasn't the extra money that convinced me. I had already made up my mind I was going to accept their offer anyway. A few days later I was on an airplane flying to Tigertown in Lakeland, Florida.

After a few weeks of extended spring training, I was sent to Bristol, Virginia, the Tigers' affiliate in the Appalachian Rookie League. One of my teammates there was a rather kooky but likable pitcher from Massachusetts named Mark Fidrych, who would later gain fame as "the Bird."

At Bristol, I played in 68 games, mostly at third base and some in the outfield but not one inning as a catcher. I struggled big time with the bat. It was my first introduction to *breaking ball, breaking ball, breaking ball*. That's all I ever saw. I was frustrated, and I hit only .213, though I did hit 11 home runs.

After the season, I was sent to the Instructional League, where the Tigers' farm director, Hoot Evers, told me that my days as a third baseman and outfielder were over. From then on, I was going to be a catcher exclusively, which was just fine with me. Then Evers said, "And we want you to switch-hit."

What?

"If you can ever get the hang of hitting left-handed," he said, "with that short porch in right field in Detroit, there's no telling how many home runs you'll hit."

So I went from playing third base and batting right-handed in rookie ball to catching every day and switch-hitting the next season in the Class A Florida State League. Even though I had caught games from Little League to high school, my first full year catching every day as a professional was in Lakeland, Florida—a different situation altogether. It was so hot and humid, it was like catching in a sauna. I never sweated so much in my life. On top of that, I was trying to learn to switch-hit, so it was a challenging year for me. I batted only .220, hit five home runs, drove in 37 runs, and struck out 85 times in 100 games.

After that season, I was sent back to the Instructional League. That's when a former major league catcher and longtime minor league manager named Les Moss, who was running the Tigers' Instructional League team, came into my life. The next year Moss would be managing Montgomery in the Class AA Southern League, likely to be my next stop up the ladder. Midway through that season, Moss told me, "That's the end of your switch-hitting."

Again, I was stunned.

"I'm just getting the hang of this," I protested. "I'm just starting to get comfortable hitting left-handed."

"You have too much power right-handed to be messing around left-handed," he said.

I went from playing third base and batting right-handed one year to catching and switch-hitting and not facing a right-handed pitcher from the right side the next year and then back around to batting exclusively right-handed the year after that. Amazingly, even though I wasn't hitting, I kept going right up the ladder in the minor league system. If I was playing in today's game, the way my batting average was, I would never have gotten out of A ball. But Hoot Evers kept moving me up.

In 1976, my third year as a professional, I was sent to Montgomery. For the first part of the season, I struggled greatly. I was back to hitting right-handed full time, but I hadn't seen a right-handed breaking ball for more than a year. I was a mess. I kept pulling everything. That's when Les Moss took over.

When we were playing at home, Les would have us go out for early hitting, and when I say, "early hitting," I mean 10:00 in the morning after a night game. We'd play the game, and when it was over Les posted a list of guys that had to report the next morning for batting practice. My name was always on the list. Always! It never came off. So, every day, when we were at home, I'd catch a night game (almost all of our home games were at night) and I'd have to get up early the next morning and get to the ballpark by 10:00 to work on my hitting.

Les would soft toss and I'd hit with two hands, and then I'd hit with one hand, first my lead hand and then my back hand. He also had a drill using a curveball machine. To keep it interesting, he made a little game of the drill. He'd point to the gaps in left-center and right-center, where they had the distances posted on the fence. He would say, "Your objective is to hit the ball between left-center field and right-center field. You can't pull the ball. You have to hit everything up the middle. As long as you hit the ball between those two boundaries, you can stay in and take another swing. But as soon as you foul a ball off or hit it to one side of the boundary or the other, you have to get out of the cage and let the next guy hit and wait your turn to hit again."

For the longest time, I'd take one swing and, boom, out of the cage. Somebody else would get in and take five, six, seven, 10 swings. I'd get in, take one swing, and out I'd go. I was so frustrated and embarrassed, until I finally started getting the hang of it, being able to direct the ball up the middle. Then I really started to drive the ball up the middle. It took a while for me to get there, but eventually I started to hit the ball out of the park over the center-field fence off the curveball machine.

I worked on my offense when the team was home. When we were on the road and we didn't have access to the field for early hitting, I'd work on my defense. Les would take me down to the corner of the outfield and work with me on shifting my weight and blocking balls in the dirt.

I started to hit a little better in the latter part of the season, but things really began to kick in the next year at Evansville in the Class AAA American Association. Moss moved up to manage Evansville, and I moved up with him. There we continued with the same drills, both offense and defense. Then all of a sudden, I started to look like I knew what I was doing swinging the bat. I always could hit for power, but making consistent contact was the problem. Once I got to Triple A, I finally started to figure things out. All that work we had done started to pay off.

In 115 games with Evansville, I batted .279, hit 25 homers, and drove in 90 runs. The Tigers called me up in September, and after that I stayed up in the big leagues. It was all because of the work I did with Les Moss, which is why

I always say that if Les had not been in the Tigers organization—and in my life—I probably never would have made it.

Since I have cleared up one misconception, let me try to clear up a couple of others that have followed me around for more than 30 years.

1. I am not related to Larry Parrish, who was an outstanding third baseman for the Montreal Expos, Texas Rangers, and Boston Red Sox in the 1970s and 1980s.
2. I was not Tina Turner's bodyguard, at least not exactly.

I can't tell you how many times over the years people have approached me and asked, "How's your brother doing?"

"What brother?" I'd say. "I don't have a brother."

"Your brother Larry."

And time and time again, I'd have to explain it.

I used to get his fan mail, and he used to get mine. Sometimes I'd check out his box scores. He might have done the same with me. I guess I was curious how he was listed. I was "Ln Parrish" and he was "La Parrish."

For years I never even met him because he played the first eight years of his career in the National League, and I was in the American League. We finally met, I think, at the All-Star Game. I was in the lobby of a hotel with my wife, and Larry was there with his wife. I didn't even know who he was until somebody introduced us. We both had the same reaction: "Oh, so *this* is what you look like." We exchanged similar stories and shared a few laughs about being mistaken as siblings.

Later, in 1999, the Tigers brought me back as a coach. And who was the manager at the time? None other than "La Parrish!" I coached for him for one season and, of course, I got his phone calls on the road, and he got mine.

Being Tina Turner's bodyguard is simply a molehill turned into a mountain. Yes, I was a bodyguard for Tina Turner—for one day only. It doesn't exactly make me Kevin Costner to Whitney Houston (as in the movie *The Bodyguard*).

After I had played a few years in the minor leagues, I got a call during the off-season from my financial adviser. He also represented George Foreman, Kareem Abdul-Jabbar, and some other big-name people, including show-business personalities. He asked me, "How would you like to come to Hollywood and be a bodyguard for Tina Turner?"

I thought he was kidding. What did I know about being a bodyguard? Didn't he know it was my dad, not me, who was in law enforcement?

"You wouldn't really have to do anything," he said. "Besides, you're not doing anything anyway except hanging out. It might be fun for you to rub elbows with some stars."

"Exactly what do I have to do?" I asked.

He explained that Tina Turner and her husband, Ike, were going through a messy divorce. Tina was filming *Hollywood Squares* in Burbank, and she wanted somebody to walk her from her dressing room to the set in case Ike showed up and made a scene.

I told him, "I don't have any training at this sort of thing, I don't know what might happen—I don't know if Ike could get violent—and you want me to go down and be her bodyguard?"

"Nothing's going to happen," he said. "You'll probably have a good time, more than anything."

I was intrigued, so I agreed to do it. I went to the studio, and the next thing I knew I was meeting Tina Turner. My job was to stand outside her dressing room when she wasn't on the set and to accompany her to the set when she was ready to film the show. After they finished taping the show, I walked her back to her dressing room.

That was it. I was there for about three hours, and the time I spent with Tina was less than 10 minutes. When I was done, I went home. I didn't get paid for it, and I never did it again. But I made the mistake of mentioning it to some of my teammates at spring training, and the thing took on a life of its own. Writers started coming around asking me about my experiences as Tina Turner's bodyguard.

Bodyguard? Hey, I didn't do anything except walk with her to and from her dressing room. I did it for a day, it was a kick, and that was the end of that. The truth is, Tina Turner wouldn't know me today if she fell over me in the street.

When I first got to Detroit in September 1977, I was just a few months past my 21st birthday, rather naïve, and, at the time, ignorant of the Tigers' incredible legacy. Growing up, I wasn't a big baseball fan. I was so involved in playing my own games, baseball, football, and basketball, that there wasn't any time to follow the big leagues. And growing up in California, I knew very little about the teams in the East, except for those that I saw on *The Game of the Week*. I don't remember ever seeing the Tigers.

When I did watch Major League Baseball, it was mainly to study techniques, especially the catchers'. My guy, the one I tried to pattern myself after, was Johnny Bench. He popularized the use of the hinged catcher's mitt. He was a one-handed catcher who tried to get his throwing hand out of the way to protect it. I liked that style, and obviously he was a great catcher and hitter, so I tried to incorporate his mechanics into my own own play.

Later I became good friends with Bench. In fact, he was a big help to me. Ordinarily, you wouldn't get to spend any time with players in the other league. You might play against them in spring training, but there usually wasn't much of an opportunity to mingle with them. There wasn't inter-league play in those early days, either. But the Tigers and the Reds played an annual sandlot benefit game, alternating yearly between Cincinnati and Detroit. When Sparky Anderson was our manager, we got a chance to visit with some of the Reds, and I got to talk with Bench.

One time I mentioned to him that I had caught a ball and hyperextended the thumb on my catching hand. I told him I just couldn't get rid of the soreness in the joint. Johnny said, "I have the answer for you. Come with me."

He took me to the Reds' training room and introduced me to the trainers, who had a sheet of rubbery material about a quarter of an inch thick. When it's put into scalding hot water, it becomes pliable. Johnny asked the trainer to make me a thumb guard. He stuck it in the hydroculator, and after a couple of minutes he extracted it, molded it around my thumb, then trimmed it and rounded off the edges. The guard went from the top of my thumb to the bottom joint and prevented me from bending it. So when I caught a ball on the tip of my thumb, the guard would keep the thumb from bending back. It took a while for me to get comfortable with it, but I didn't have another problem with my thumb for the remainder of my career. Thank you, Johnny Bench—it was a lifesaver.

After spending as much time in Detroit as I did, I came to appreciate its great baseball tradition and how many legendary players were Tigers. In researching my all-time Tigers team, what struck me was the number of players who spent their entire major league careers with the team (including Charlie Gehringer, Hooks Dauss, Al Kaline, Tommy Bridges, Alan Trammell, Lou Whitaker, John Hiller, and Bill Freehan) and the number of Tigers who grew up in Detroit (Hal Newhouser, Ron LeFlore, Willie Horton, and Freehan) and Michigan (Gehringer, Kirk Gibson, and Charlie Maxwell).

When it came to making my selections for the all-time Tigers team, I am pleased that most of my choices were guys with deep Tigers roots. I didn't plan it; that's just how it worked out.

You might think some players—in particular, Mickey Cochrane, Goose Goslin, and George Kell, all Hall of Famers—should be higher on my list. But in making my choices, I gave greater weight to a player's performance as a Tiger than to the sum total of his career. Most of the outstanding accomplishments of these three great players came with teams other than the Tigers.

This is not an official team selected by the Tigers, the fans, or a panel of experts. It's strictly my team. I hope I got it right and that I have not slighted, undervalued, or overlooked anyone. If I did, I apologize.

—Lance Parrish

Acknowledgments

I affectionately and gratefully acknowledge my four managers and 154 team-mates, the trainers, clubhouse personnel and front-office staff, and the thousands of fans who supported us in my 10 years with the Detroit Tigers.

I also am indebted to Al Kaline, Rusty Staub, Sparky Anderson, Gary Carter, and Charlie Maxwell for their generous contributions to this book; to John Boggs; and to the good folks at Triumph Books for affording me the rare opportunity to add the word "author" to my resume.

Introduction

The Tigers of Detroit almost died in infancy, but they survived a near-death experience to become one of the American League's most formidable and stable (albeit conservative) franchises for more than a century, winning 10 pennants and four World Series and producing some of baseball's most illustrious stars.

Through the years, Tigers players have won 22 batting titles, 11 home run crowns, 19 RBI titles, nine Most Valuable Player awards, three Cy Young Awards, four Rookie of the Year awards, and 37 Gold Gloves.

Tigers manager Bill Armour was the first to employ extensive use of platooning players, in 1906, but the Tigers were also the next-to-last team in Major League Baseball to install lights, in 1948, and the next-to-last to field a black player, in 1958, 11 years after Jackie Robinson broke baseball's color line.

Mention the Tigers, and the names Cobb, Heilmann, Gehringer, Cochrane, Greenberg, Newhouser, Kaline, Kell, Trammel, Horton, and Whitaker readily come to mind.

Although fans are justifiably proud of the rich tradition of their Tigers, at the same time they cannot help but lament what might have been. A team that can boast some of the greatest hitters baseball has known, unfortunately, due to bad judgment, rarely has been able to support those hitters with pitchers of comparable stature. Imagine how the baseball landscape might have changed had the Tigers not traded away such pitching luminaries as:

- Eddie Cicotte: Signed by Detroit, he appeared in three games for the Tigers in 1905, winning one and losing one, and then was returned to the minor leagues. The Red Sox purchased him from Lincoln in the Western League for $2,500 before the 1908 season. He went on to win 208 games and lose 149 for the Red Sox and White Sox, including a phenomenal 29–7 in 1919, the year of the "Black Sox" scandal. A year later, Cicotte and seven of his White Sox teammates were banned from baseball for life for their part in throwing the World Series to Cincinnati.

   Ironically, once out of baseball, he returned to Detroit to work for the Ford Motor Company and remained there until he died, 50 years after the Black Sox scandal.

- Howard Ehmke: The submarine-baller won 75 games in six seasons with the Tigers and then was traded after the 1922 season to the Red Sox with three other players and $25,000 for infielder Del Pratt and pitcher Rip Collins. In the next seven seasons, he would win 91 more games for the Red Sox and Athletics, while Collins won 44 games in five seasons with the Tigers.

- Carl Hubbell: He was purchased by the Tigers from Oklahoma City in 1925 and spent three mediocre years pitching in the Tigers' farm system. The Tigers brought him to spring training in 1928, but manager Ty Cobb didn't like what he saw in Hubbell and forbade him to throw his screwball. It would later become his signature pitch.

   The Tigers outrighted Hubbell to Beaumont in the Texas League, where a scout for the New York Giants spotted him and urged Giants manager John McGraw to purchase him.

   With the Giants, Hubbell won 253 games; won more than 20 games for five consecutive seasons; twice was voted National League MVP; earned everlasting fame by striking out in succession future Hall of Famers Babe Ruth, Lou Gehrig, Jimmie Foxx, Al Simmons, and Joe Cronin in the 1934 All-Star Game; and was elected to the Hall of Fame.

- Billy Pierce: Signed as an amateur free agent in 1945, he pitched in 27 games for the Tigers and then was traded to the Chicago White Sox in 1948 with $10,000 for catcher Aaron Robinson, who played in 253 games for the Tigers over two and a half seasons. In 16 seasons with the White Sox and Giants, Pierce won 208 games.

- John Smoltz: Selected in the 22ⁿᵈ round in the June 1985 free-agent draft, he never pitched for the Tigers. He was traded on August 12, 1987, to the Atlanta Braves for veteran Doyle Alexander.

  Alexander was 9–0 for the Tigers down the stretch in 1987 and helped them win a division title, but three years later, he was out of baseball. Meanwhile, Smoltz completed his 21ˢᵗ major league season in 2009. Moving from a starting pitcher to a closer and back again, he had won 210 games, saved 154 games, and struck out more than 3,000 batters.

The Tigers were charter members of the American League in 1901, joining teams from Chicago, Boston, Philadelphia, Baltimore, Washington, Cleveland, and Milwaukee to form the junior circuit as a rival to the established National League. Managed by George Stallings, who would later gain fame as manager of the New York Highlanders and the 1914 "Miracle Braves," Detroit played its first game on April 25, 1901, against Milwaukee. In a portent of the style of play that would become a franchise trademark, the Tigers entered the bottom of the ninth trailing 13–4 and staged an unlikely 10-run rally to pull out a stunning 14–13 victory that delighted the crowd of almost 12,000 in Detroit's 6,000-seat Bennett Park.

Two theories have been advanced for the name "Tigers." Stallings took credit for the nickname, claiming he called his team "Tigers" in 1896 when, playing in the minor Western League, he outfitted his players in black-and-yellow striped socks.

Other sources attribute the name to Detroit *Free Press* sports editor Philip Reid, who noted that the color of the socks worn by Detroit players was similar to the uniforms worn by athletes at Princeton University, also the Tigers.

Vehemently disapproving of Stallings' incessant bombastic and invective-laced tirades against rival players and umpires, American League president Ban Johnson attempted to oust the Tigers from Detroit and his league in 1903 and move them to Pittsburgh in the National League, which fought to block the move. Ultimately, a compromise was reached. The Tigers would stay in Detroit in exchange for the senior National League's recognition and acceptance of the upstart new league and granting the American League permission to move its Baltimore franchise to New York, where the senior circuit had a stronghold with the established New York Giants.

Soon after the turn of the 20th century, the city of Detroit, home of the automobile industry, experienced amazing growth as Americans became fascinated with the use of "horseless carriages." The Tigers were the unwitting beneficiaries of this new fad. Baseball was the workingman's pastime, the blue-collar sport, and Detroit became the prototypical blue-collar city.

After finishing third, seventh, fifth, seventh, third, and sixth in their first six years, the Tigers' fortunes turned first with the arrival of an 18-year-old outfielder from Narrows, Georgia, named Tyrus Raymond Cobb in 1905, and two years later, Hughie Jennings—who was winding down an illustrious playing career with Louisville, Baltimore, Brooklyn, and Philadelphia—as manager.

Jennings would lead the Tigers to the American League pennant in each of his first three years, losing in the World Series twice to the Cubs and once to the Pirates. He would remain as manager for 14 seasons, finishing in the first division of the eight-team league 10 times.

After winning the American League pennant in 1909, the Tigers would go 25 years before winning again. In the eight seasons from 1926 to 1933, the Tigers would finish in the second division seven times under managers Ty Cobb, George Moriarty, and Bucky Harris, despite the arrival in 1933 of a muscular, power-hitting, 6'4", 210-pound rookie first baseman named Henry Benjamin (Hammerin' Hank) Greenberg.

Greenberg, who broke into the American League with a .301 average, 12 home runs, and 87 RBI, had been raised in the Bronx, New York, practically in the shadow of Yankee Stadium. The Yankees had recruited him heavily, but noticing that the incumbent first baseman in the Bronx, Lou Gehrig, was still in his twenties, Greenberg eschewed the overtures of his hometown team and signed with the Tigers.

Two games before the end of the 1933 season, with a second consecutive fifth-place finish and the Tigers' fourth sub-.500 season in five years assured, Harris resigned as manager.

With attendance having plummeted from a high of 1,015,136 in 1924 to a shockingly low 320,972, owner Frank Navin determined that the Tigers needed not only a personnel overhaul but a strong box-office personality to draw fans back to the ballpark. And in 1933, there was no greater personality in all of sports than the mighty Babe Ruth.

At age 38, the incomparable Babe still put up impressive numbers in '33, but it was evident that he was nearing the end of his fabulous career. His batting average of .301 was down 40 points from the previous season. His home runs fell off from 41 to 34, his RBI from 137 to 103. Babe had made it known that he had a strong desire to manage a big-league team. He never hid his disappointment when, in 1931, the Yankees named Joe McCarthy their manager after Miller Huggins died and Bob Shawkey was found wanting in his one-year trial at the job.

Convinced that Ruth was just the man to restore the Tigers to prominence and, more important, to bring back the fans, Navin offered Babe the job of managing his team. It was a tempting offer but a difficult decision for the Babe, who believed he still had another year or two remaining as a productive and highly paid player.

Ruth wrestled with his decision, but those close to him believed he was leaning toward accepting the Tigers' offer. He asked Navin for a little time to think it over and said he would meet with the Detroit owner after he had fulfilled a commitment for a series of personal appearances in Hawaii.

As it turned out, Ruth would learn the valuable lesson that he who hesitates is lost. While the Babe was funning and sunning in Hawaii, Navin was confronted with a decision of his own. At the time, Connie Mack, his team in financial straits, was in the process of dismantling his once mighty Philadelphia Athletics, and Navin had the opportunity to purchase the contract of Gordon (Mickey) Cochrane for $100,000. Cochrane, still only 30 years old, had spent nine seasons with the Athletics, had a lifetime batting average of .321, and he was coming off a season in which he batted .322. Navin not only jumped at the chance to acquire Cochrane but, although he had never managed, decided to make Cochrane the Tigers' player/manager.

Cochrane was an immediate success on the field, in the dugout, and at the box office. In 129 games, he batted .320 and drove in 76 runs. He improved the Tigers by 26 games to a record of 101–53. Led by the "G Men," Hank Greenberg, Charlie Gehringer, and Goose Goslin (who was acquired from Washington in a trade)—all future Hall of Famers—Cochrane guided the Tigers to their first pennant in 25 years. And he helped triple the team's home attendance. A year later, the Tigers repeated as American League champions and defeated the Cubs in six games to win their first World Series.

Cochrane would manage for four more seasons without reaching the heights he attained in his first two years. The Tigers would go seven more years without winning a pennant until they prevailed in 1945 under manager Steve O'Neill in a weakened American League when many of baseball's biggest stars (Hank Greenberg included) were off serving their country during World War II.

With draft-deferred left-hander Hal Newhouser leading the way, the Tigers finished a game and a half ahead of Washington and beat the Cubs in seven games to win their second World Series. Newhouser won 25 games during the regular season—two more in the World Series—and captured his second consecutive Most Valuable Player award.

The Tigers would go 23 years under 11 different managers before winning another pennant.

The most notable addition to the Tigers in that 23-year period was an 18-year-old bonus baby named Al Kaline, signed out of a Baltimore high school. Kaline made his debut with the Tigers on June 25, 1953, and spent his entire 22-year career as a Tiger without ever spending a day in the minor leagues. He had a career batting average of .297, hit 399 home runs, drove in 1,583 runs, won 10 Gold Gloves, and was elected to the Hall of Fame in 1980.

With a sixth-place finish in 1960 and their 15th straight season without a pennant under eight different managers, change was in the wind for the Tigers. Joe Gordon—who had replaced Jimmy Dykes for the final 57 games of the season in a bizarre trade of managers (Dykes went to Cleveland, Gordon to Detroit)—was let go, and the Tigers began the search for his replacement.

Their first choice was the venerable Casey Stengel, who had been "resigned" by the Yankees for the unpardonable sin of reaching the age of 70 after winning 10 pennants and seven World Series in 12 years. The deal was set. The Tigers wanted Stengel and Stengel wanted to continue managing, but his doctors strongly advised the "Ol' Perfessor" against returning to work.

Thwarted in their attempt to attach themselves to some Yankees magic, the Tigers turned to former catcher Bob Scheffing. With such stars as Kaline, Norm Cash, Rocky Colavito, Bill Bruton, Frank Lary, and Jim Bunning, the Tigers were a powerhouse team that won 101 games, the most by a Tigers team in 27 years. Unfortunately, that was the year of the Yankees' M&M Boys

(Roger Maris and Mickey Mantle), who combined for 115 home runs and led the Yankees to 109 victories and an eight-game margin over the Tigers.

In the next 20 years, the Tigers would win only two titles—in 1968 when Denny McLain, baseball's last 30-game winner, won 31 games and the Tigers posted 103 victories under Mayo Smith. They finished 12 games ahead of the Orioles and beat the Cardinals in seven games in the World Series. In 1972 they won the AL East but lost to Oakland in the American League Championship Series under Billy Martin, who exhibited what would become a trend by dramatically improving the Tigers immediately and then wearing out his welcome and getting fired after only two and a half seasons.

The Tigers ushered in a new era in 1979 when they named Sparky Anderson as manager, who had been unceremoniously let go by the Cincinnati Reds the previous year after nine seasons during which he won five division titles, four National League pennants, and two World Series and finished lower than second place just once.

Anderson remained with the Tigers for 17 years, during which he won a pennant and the World Series in 1984 and a division title in 1987.

When Anderson retired, the Tigers suffered through 10 consecutive losing seasons until Jim Leyland arrived in 2006, improved the team by 24 games, and won the Tigers' 10th pennant as the American League wild-card team.

In winning four World Series, it is not surprising that the Tigers were led by three outstanding catchers—Hall of Famer Mickey Cochrane, who doubled as manager, in 1935; 11-time All-Star Bill Freehan in 1968; and eight-time All-Star and three-time Gold Glove winner Lance Parrish in 1984.

Parrish would spend 10 seasons with the Tigers and later would serve two three-year tours as a Tigers coach under managers Larry Parrish, Phil Garner, and Alan Trammell, and one year as a television color commentator on Tigers games.

Parrish has played with, coached, and become acquainted with many of the greats who wore a Tigers uniform. As such, he is uniquely qualified for the difficult challenge of selecting the five players at each position and the managers who make up his all-time Tigers team.

—Phil Pepe

ONE

Catcher

This is not a misprint, and it's not evidence of my ignorance of baseball history. I know Mickey Cochrane is in the Hall of Fame, Pudge Rodriguez will be once he becomes eligible, and Bill Freehan is not. I know Cochrane had a lifetime batting average of .320 and that he hit over .300 nine times, that Rodriguez is hovering around .300 lifetime and has hit over .300 10 times, whereas Freehan had a lifetime batting average of .262 and batted .300 just once.

But the objective here is not to pick an all-time team, but to pick my all-time *Tigers* team. Cochrane played for the Tigers only four of his 13 major league seasons (the other nine were spent with the Philadelphia Athletics). Rodriguez made his name, for the most part, with the Texas Rangers; he was a Tiger for only five of his almost 20 major league seasons. Freehan was "Mr. Michigan." He spent his entire 15-year career with the Tigers.

So **Bill Freehan** is my choice as the No. 1 catcher in Tigers history because of his longevity with the team—and I'll take the flak from those who would

1.	BILL FREEHAN
2.	IVAN RODRIGUEZ
3.	MICKEY COCHRANE
4.	MICKEY TETTLETON
5.	MATT NOKES

A Michigan native, Bill Freehan spent his entire career with the Tigers. He held the major league record for catchers in fielding percentage for more than three decades.

disagree. Actually, I don't feel I have to apologize for picking Freehan as the Tigers' No. 1 catcher—that's how good he was.

Besides, Freehan is a hometown guy. A Detroit native, he was a football and baseball star at the University of Michigan (and when his playing career was over, he went back and coached his alma mater's baseball team from 1990–95) who was signed out of college by the Tigers for the then-princely sum of $100,000.

That was in 1961. Two years later, Bill took over as the Tigers' No. 1 catcher at the age of 21 and kept the job for the next 14 seasons, except for 1974, when he played more games at first base than at catcher. After he became the Tigers' regular catcher, he was a fixture there, making the All-Star team 10 straight years, seven as a starter. He even had the honor of catching a pop-up off the bat of Tim McCarver for the final out of the 1968 World Series, which is entirely fitting because Bill was, and is, one of the most popular players in Tigers history.

I admit to being slightly biased where Freehan is concerned. Bill was still the Tigers' No. 1 catcher as I was coming up through their farm system in the mid-1970s. After his career ended in 1976, he would come down to spring training and work with the catchers, so naturally he worked with me quite a bit. The Tigers made me his pet project. He spent a lot of time with me in the bullpen and on the field working on mechanics, so he sort of became my personal instructor and mentor. I learned a lot from him.

As a young guy trying to soak up knowledge, having a guy like Bill Freehan there to learn from, with all he has accomplished in the game, gave a big boost to my development. One thing was especially helpful: Bill and I are about the same height—he's 6'2" and I'm 6'3"—and I struggled to find a comfortable stance behind the plate. I never knew if I was low enough, nor did I ever get confirmation from anyone that I had a proper stance until Bill started working with me.

Bill made good suggestions, like getting me to spread my feet more, and he would always tell me if I was doing things right. Getting that reassurance that I was on the right track from someone like him, such an outstanding catcher, was a great boost for my confidence.

All of the pitchers I talked to for whom Freehan caught, including Mickey Lolich, John Hiller, and Hank Aguirre, had nothing but great things to say about Bill. They praised his ability to handle a pitching staff, to call a game, to set up hitters, and to stay on the same page about pitch selection throughout the course of the game. From what they said, he was a very good glove man who rarely dropped anything, which I found interesting, because Bill used one of those old "no break" gloves. When I was in high school, I played with one. It was like a big, round pillow with a little pocket. Unless your glove was really broken in, you needed to catch two-handed. But these guys—Lolich, Hiller, and Aguirre—just raved about Freehan's hands, how soft they were and how well he handled pitchers.

All of that is supported by his statistics. Freehan led the American League in putouts six times and in fielding average three times, and he won five Gold

Gloves. When he retired, he had a career fielding percentage of .9333, a major league record for catchers that lasted for almost 30 years. He also had major league records for career putouts and total chances that would last for more than 10 years, and he was ninth in major league history in games caught.

As a hitter, Freehan finished with 200 homers and 2,502 total bases, placing him third all-time among American League catchers at his retirement.

On the Tigers' all-time list, Bill is 10th in games played and at-bats and ninth in home runs. He also holds a couple of Tigers records I'm sure he'd rather not have. He's their all-time leader for a single season and a career in getting hit by a pitch.

Five years after he retires (if he ever does retire), **Ivan "Pudge" Rodriguez** will be elected to the National Baseball Hall of Fame, in all likelihood in his first year of eligibility. It will be an honor and distinction that is richly deserved.

What Mickey Cochrane and Gabby Hartnett were to the 1920s and 1930s, Bill Dickey was to the 1940s, Yogi Berra and Roy Campanella were to the 1950s, Johnny Bench and Carlton Fisk were to the 1970s, and Fisk and Gary Carter were to the 1980s, Pudge Rodriguez is to the 1990s and 2000s—the standard by which all catchers are measured.

Pudge is a pretty amazing catcher. As far as numbers go, there are not too many guys who can compete with him—in offense as well as defense.

I remember watching Pudge when he came up with Texas in the early 1990s. He was a pretty good hitter, but the thing that stood out to everybody was his defensive skill, especially in throwing. Hitters just couldn't steal off him, and they couldn't get too far off base or they would be picked off.

The thing that baseball people talk about when they look at a catcher is footwork. When you're throwing the ball to second base or you're trying to pick a runner off first, the movement of your feet is a big determinant in how fast your throw will get there. I have always said that Pudge had the quickest feet of any catcher I have ever seen.

In 1999, when Rodriguez won the American League's Most Valuable Player award playing for Texas, somebody asked me about him, and I said, "This guy, when he's behind the plate, has a chance to control the tempo of

Pudge Rodriguez's stellar fielding and robust offensive numbers make a convincing argument for a first-ballot Hall of Fame selection.

the game and control the opposition's running game. He's that good. Guys are afraid to get off first base too far, they don't get good leads, and that lends itself to runners not stealing second base too often. And if they do try to steal, he has an excellent chance of throwing them out. His percentage of throwing runners out is pretty phenomenal [Editor's note: Rodriguez has a 47 percent success rate at throwing runners out attempting to steal. By comparison, Carlton Fisk threw out 34 percent of runners attempting to steal, Gary Carter 35 percent, and Johnny Bench 43 percent.] Pudge has the ability to singlehandedly shut down a team's running game."

When Rodriguez left Detroit late in the 2008 season, he had made the All-Star team 14 times, 12 times as the starting catcher, and he had won 13 Gold Gloves, the most of any catcher ever and three more than Bench.

And I haven't even talked about his offense yet. Besides the .300 lifetime batting average and 10 seasons over .300—eight in a row from 1995–2002—he has a higher lifetime average than Bench, Berra, Campanella, Carter, Fisk, and Hartnett; more home runs that Campanella, Cochrane, Dickey, and Hartnett; and more RBI than Campanella, Carter, Cochrane, Dickey, and Hartnett. And he's still playing.

Is Pudge a Hall of Famer? Without a doubt. I would be shocked if he isn't elected on the first ballot.

Mickey Cochrane is one of the greatest (many say *the* greatest) catchers ever to play the game. I'm not disputing that fact. He was the third catcher elected to the Hall of Fame, is one of only 13 catchers enshrined in Cooperstown, and at the time he retired, his lifetime batting average of .320 was the highest ever for a catcher.

So why isn't he No. 1 on my list of all-time Tigers catchers?

Simple. Most of Cochrane's best years came before he arrived in Detroit in 1934. In nine seasons with the Philadelphia Athletics, he batted over .300 six times and only once batted lower than .293. He was a left-handed, line-drive hitter who ran well enough for Athletics manager Connie Mack to use him as his leadoff hitter. Cochrane hit 59 triples for the A's and stole 50 bases.

In 1934, his first year with the Tigers, Cochrane batted .320, drove in 76 runs, and was named American League MVP for the second time (he won as a member of the Athletics in 1928). Thereafter his offense declined. In his four seasons in Detroit, Cochrane batted .313 but had only 11 home runs and 152 RBI.

Mickey Cochrane's .320 career batting average stood for more than 70 years as the major league record among catchers, until Joe Mauer came along.

Cochrane's time in Detroit as a manager is more noteworthy. In his first two years, he won back-to-back pennants and one World Series. In his next two years, he finished second.

I'll talk more about Mickey Cochrane in Chapter 12.

Mickey Tettleton had a very productive 14-year major league career with four teams, including four years with the Tigers. He signed some lucrative contracts in the free-agent era, but he probably could have made much more money than he did if someone would have had the good sense to employ him as a spokesman for Kellogg's Froot Loops cereal.

*H*umility prevents Lance Parrish from including himself among the top five catchers in Detroit Tigers history or to suggest that his major league career was Hall of Fame worthy. So it is left for others, and for the numbers, to plead Parrish's case for him.

Left to a disinterested jury, where would Parrish rate among Tigers catchers? Certainly in the top five! But how high up on that list?

It would be foolhardy to suggest that, based on the totality of their careers, Parrish rates ahead of Mickey Cochrane, the only catcher in the Hall of Fame to have worn a Detroit uniform, or Pudge Rodriguez, who eventually will join that exalted Cooperstown fraternity.

However, based solely on his accomplishments in Detroit, guidelines set by Parrish himself in selecting his all-time Tigers' team, Parrish is likely no lower than No. 2 on the all-time list of Tigers catchers. You be the judge:

	Years	Games	Hits	HR	RBI	BA
Bill Freehan	1961–76	1,774	1,591	200	758	.262
Pudge Rodriguez	2004–08	611	709	62	300	.298
Mickey Cochrane	1934–37	315	335	11	152	.313
Mickey Tettleton	1991–94	570	469	112	333	.249
Matt Nokes	1986–90	395	334	61	189	.268
Lance Parrish	**1977–86**	**1,146**	**1,123**	**212**	**700**	**.263**

Parrish reached the Tigers for 12 games at age 21 in 1977, played in 85 games in 1978, and took over as their No. 1 catcher in 1979.

"Parrish was just settling in as the Tigers' No. 1 catcher when I left Detroit," remembered Rusty Staub. "He was an Adonis. Nobody was built any better than he was. I missed his best years, but he turned out to be a hell of a catcher. He not only hit, he did a good job behind the plate; He's a fine guy. I really liked him a lot. He wasn't swell-headed, and I found him to be very intelligent. He was one of the people I was sorry I didn't get to know better before I left Detroit."

While with the Tigers, Parrish would win three Gold Gloves and make the All-Star team six times, twice as the American League's starting catcher.

His best season was 1982 when he batted .284 and belted 32 home runs, breaking the American League record for home runs by a catcher, which had been set by Yogi Berra in 1956 with 30 and tied by Gus Triandos two years later. To his surprise, Parrish received a telegram from Berra congratulating him on breaking the record. Parrish framed the telegram and still displays it in his den.

In 1984, Parrish raised the record to 33, but a year later Carlton Fisk belted 37 homers to claim the AL record.

"Berra had the record for almost 30 years," said Parrish. "I had it for three."

Three catchers who were contemporaries of Lance Parrish are currently enshrined in the Baseball Hall of Fame in Cooperstown, New York, among them Johnny Bench, believed by many to be the greatest catcher in the history of the game.

This is not to say that Parrish deserves to be elected to the Hall of Fame (when he became eligible for his name to appear on the ballot in 2001, he received nine votes, or 1.7 percent; Freehan, in 1982, received two votes or .5 percent, Tettleton and Nokes received no votes), but it is interesting to see how Parrish compares with his three Hall of Fame contemporaries:

	Games*	Hits	HR	RBI	BA
Johnny Bench	2,158	2,048	389	1,376	.267
Gary Carter	2,295	2,092	324	1,225	.262
Carlton Fisk	2,499	2,356	376	1,330	.269
Lance Parrish	**1,988**	**1,782**	**324**	**1,070**	**.252**

*—Includes games played at other positions, as a designated hitter, and pinch-hitter.

Although their major league careers overlapped for 16 years, Parrish and Gary Carter played in the same league for only two seasons, 1987 and 1988—Parrish with the Philadelphia Phillies, Carter with the New York Mets—and it wasn't until they met socially on trips sponsored by Nike that they formed a relationship and discovered how much they shared in common:

• They were born within 27 months of each other: Carter on April 8, 1954, Parrish on June 15, 1956.

• They grew up within 30 miles of each other in Southern California.

- Carter turned down a football scholarship at UCLA to sign with the Montreal Expos; Parrish turned down a football scholarship at UCLA to sign with the Detroit Tigers.
- Carter was an infielder who was drafted by the Expos as a catcher; Parrish was a catcher who was drafted by the Tigers as an infielder.

"Lance and I hit it off on those Nike trips and so did our wives," said Carter. "I have nothing but good things to say about Lance. We still exchange Christmas cards, and my wife Sandy and I always comment on what a great looking family they have, to the point that they could be on some model magazine together."

Carter retired three years before Parrish, but because of their relationship, Carter continued to follow Parrish's career and noted that he and Parrish finished with the same number of home runs, 324—five ahead of Cecil Fielder, one behind Willie Horton, and seven behind Hank Greenberg.

"I've always wondered why he didn't get more consideration for the Hall of Fame," said Carter.

* * *

Lance Parrish

Parrish was three days short of his 23rd birthday and in his first full season with the Tigers when Sparky Anderson arrived in Detroit, bringing with him from Cincinnati an impressive nine-year resume and the memories of having watched the emergence and maturation of the great Johnny Bench. Now the manager would have to learn to cope with the immaturity and lack of experience of a young catcher.

"Young guys, if they haven't been directed right and they haven't been told right, let's don't blame them," Anderson said. "Let's teach them. I learned in my latter years that teaching is more important than the winning part. You must teach 'em before you can win.

"Lance was just a baby when I got there. At first he was having trouble blocking balls. It really bothered him because he wanted to do good, so I told him, 'You know what I'm going to do for you, son? I'm going to put a man named Bill Freehan with you, and he could catch. I'm going to ask him if he will come to spring training and just stay with you. You'll be his pupil. I'll have no authority over you. He will have all the authority.'

"Bill agreed to come to spring training and for three years he stayed with Lance, and Bill Freehan is the one that made Lance a good catcher. He helped him physically, and he helped him mentally. You couldn't believe what a good kid Parrish was. He's such a good person beyond being so strong and wanting to learn and accepting teaching. Every time he did something wrong, he wanted to blame himself, and I said, 'Hey, I don't want no blaming.'

"He wanted to do good, not to be a star. He just wanted to be good at what he did. And he turned out to be good. You give me Lance Parrish as my catcher, and I'll be very happy."

Tettleton was originally drafted by the Oakland A's and spent four years with them as a backup catcher of little distinction before being released. He then signed on as a free agent with Baltimore and showed a little more promise in 1988, batting .261 with 11 homers and 37 RBI, platooning with Terry Kennedy.

When Kennedy left Baltimore in 1989, Mickey took over as the Orioles' No. 1 catcher. It was his breakout year. He hit 26 homers, drove in 65 runs, and was selected to the American League All-Star team. When reporters began looking for reasons behind Tettleton's sudden improvement, his wife attributed it to Mickey eating Froot Loops for breakfast.

The Froot Loops legend followed him to Detroit when he was traded to the Tigers as a free agent after the 1990 season. Over the next four years, Tettleton put up some very impressive numbers for the Tigers, including 112 home runs and 333 RBI.

I never played with Tettleton, but I played against him—and he caught my eye when he was with Baltimore. I was a fan of his hitting style, I suppose because whenever we played against him, he gave us fits. He was a switch-hitter with excellent power. I remember him behind the batter, but he also

Mickey Tettleton was a patient hitter who could hit for power. During his four years with the Tigers, he averaged more than 100 walks per season.

played first base and was a designated hitter. You never knew where you were going to see him. But I do remember thinking that when he caught, he did a good job behind the plate and he threw pretty well.

One of the things that impressed me most about him was his patience and discipline at the plate. He seemed to get 100 walks or close to it every year. He had four consecutive years, and five out of six, with more than 100 walks. He finished in the top five in walks in the American League for seven consecutive years, from 1990–96. With the Tigers in 1992, he led the American League in walks with 122, which is also sixth on Detroit's all-time list for walks in a season.

When **Matt Nokes** was coming up through the Tigers' farm system, I didn't know much about him. I first saw him in spring training, and what I saw was a pretty good-looking young catcher, a left-handed hitter who swung the bat well and had some pop. Little did I know that he would become my replacement as the Tigers' regular catcher.

After I left Detroit for Philadelphia in 1987, Nokes got his chance to be the Tigers' regular catcher, and he made the most of it. He was only 23 years old, and the numbers he put up in his first full season—a .289 average, higher than any average I had in my entire big-league career; 32 home runs, one less than I hit in 1984, my eighth season, when I briefly held the record for the most home runs by an American League catcher; 87 RBI; and selection to the All-Star team—made the Tigers and their fans forget about me in a hurry.

Matt Nokes played for four teams over nine seasons but never duplicated the success he had in his rookie season with the Tigers.

They had a young catcher who was a left-handed power hitter and had a tremendous upside. The people of Detroit hardly had a chance to notice I was
gone. Nokes picked up the slack and ran with it.

Then, just as quickly, he tailed off. In his second full season, he slipped
from a .289 average to .251, from 32 homers to 16, and from 87 RBI to 53.
The following year, he fell even farther, to a .250 average, only nine homers
and 39 RBI, and the year after that he was traded to the Yankees in June.

Whether it was simply a case of too much too soon or simply that he
needed more time in the minor leagues or as a backup to hone his skills, I
have no idea, but the fact is that Nokes played 902 major league games for five
teams in 11 seasons and, although he had a couple of pretty good power years
with the Yankees, he never again so much as came close to duplicating what
he did for the Tigers in his rookie year.

Statistical Summaries

All statistics are for player's Tigers career only.

HITTING

G = Games

H = Hits

HR = Home runs

RBI = Runs batted in

SB = Stolen bases

BA = Batting average

Catcher	Years	G	H	HR	RBI	SB	BA
Bill Freehan *Drew league-leading 15 intentional walks in 1967*	1961, 63–76	1,774	1591	200	758	24	.262
Pudge Rodriguez *Has .306 batting average in 14 All-Star Game appearances*	2004–08	611	709	62	300	30	.298
Mickey Cochrane *Hit for the cycle twice for Athletics (7/22/32, 8/2/33)*	1934–37	315	335	11	152	14	.313

continued	Years	G	H	HR	RBI	SB	BA
Mickey Tettleton *Belted pinch-hit grand slam at Yankee Stadium on 8/11/91*	1991–94	570	469	112	333	6	.249
Matt Nokes *Won Silver Slugger award as a rookie in 1987*	1986–90	395	334	61	189	3	.268

FIELDING

PO = Putouts

A = Assists

E = Errors

DP = Double plays

TC/G = Total chances divided by games played

FA = Fielding average

Catcher	PO	A	E	DP	TC/G	FA
Bill Freehan	9,941	721	72	98	6.8	.993
Pudge Rodriguez	3,500	259	27	32	6.6	.993
Mickey Cochrane	1,288	145	16	15	4.8	.988
Mickey Tettleton	1,538	141	11	14	4.9	.993
Matt Nokes	1,502	112	19	16	5.5	.988

TWO

First Baseman

One of my greatest regrets about my baseball career is that I never took advantage of the opportunity to talk hitting with **Hank Greenberg**.

I met him once, at the 1980 All-Star Game in Dodger Stadium, Los Angeles. It was my first All-Star Game, and Greenberg was the American League's honorary captain. I could kick myself…I didn't even ask him to sign a baseball. But I was still a young player, and I felt funny about asking guys like that for autographs.

It was an honor just to meet him. Obviously, playing in Detroit and coming up through the Tigers' farm system, I had heard plenty about him. We exchanged a few words of greeting (I don't even remember what) and that was kind of neat, but I didn't get to talk to him as much as I would have liked. Those All-Star Games come and go so quickly and there's so much going on that you really don't have a chance to spend a lot of time with the visiting dignitaries.

1. HANK GREENBERG

2. NORM CASH

3. RUDY YORK

4. CECIL FIELDER

5. TONY CLARK

I saw Greenberg one other time. It was in 1983, and the Tigers had invited him and Charlie Gehringer to Tiger Stadium for a ceremony to officially retire their numbers, Greenberg's No. 5 and Gehringer's No. 2. Unfortunately, they never came through the clubhouse, which was disappointing. They simply went on the field for the ceremony and were whisked away as quickly as they'd arrived.

I suppose at the time I thought that there would be other occasions when I would get the chance to talk to Greenberg, but I never did. He lived on the West Coast then, and he died three years later.

Playing in Detroit, I had heard so many great things from so many people about Greenberg, both as a tremendous player and as a man of dignity and class, that I would have enjoyed talking baseball with him, especially hitting. I have always put a higher premium on run production than batting average, and Greenberg's production was off the charts. Eight times he had a slugging percentage of .600 or better, and his career percentage of .605 is seventh all-time, ahead of Joe DiMaggio, Mickey Mantle, Willie Mays, Hank Aaron, Alex Rodriguez, Manny Ramirez, and Mark McGwire.

Some might look at Greenberg's career numbers and wonder what all the fuss is about. He hit only 331 home runs and drove in only 1,276 runs. A lot of guys had higher numbers than that, but in Greenberg's case, the numbers don't tell the whole story. He spent parts of 13 seasons in the major leagues, but in only nine seasons did he play more than 100 games, and in only six did he play in more than 140 games.

He missed all of 1942, 1943, and 1944, all but 19 games in 1941 and all but 78 games in 1945— just after his 30th birthday until just after his 34th birthday, prime years for a baseball player—to military service in World War II. He also missed all but 12 games with a broken wrist in 1936.

That's more than 800 games and approximately 5¼ seasons that Greenberg lost in service to his country and by injury during what might have been the prime of his career. What would his numbers have been if he had not lost those 800 games?

To give you an idea of what he might have accomplished in those missing years, in 1935, the year before he broke his wrist, Greenberg had 36 home runs and (gasp!) 170 RBI. In 1940, his last full season before he went off to war, Greenberg hit 41 home runs and drove in 150. A conservative estimate is that he might have averaged 35 homers and 140 RBI in those missing years, so it is not inconceivable that had he not missed those 800 games, he would have added about 185 home runs and 750 RBI to his career total, giving him 516 homers and 2,026 RBI, which, when he retired, would have placed him second on the all-time list in both categories.

Hall of Famer "Hammerin'" Hank Greenberg was a punishing batter who put up huge career numbers despite losing the prime years in his career to military service.

Greenberg was born in New York City and raised in the Bronx, practically in the shadow of Yankee Stadium. In high school, he was a big, lumbering, power-hitting first baseman who attracted a great deal of attention from major league scouts. All three New York teams had their chance to sign him. The Dodgers, in Brooklyn, never made him an offer; the Giants, owned by John McGraw, who had been looking for a Jewish player to help attract New York's large Jewish population, liked young Hank's power but felt he was too clumsy and uncoordinated and passed on signing him; the Yankees, however, made Greenberg a substantial offer.

At the time, the Yankees' lineup included Babe Ruth, Lou Gehrig, Bill Dickey, Tony Lazzeri, and Earle Combs. The thought of adding Greenberg's bat to that array—or later, pairing him with Gehrig, Dickey, and Joe DiMaggio—is staggering.

Happily (for the Tigers), Greenberg had the good sense to realize that with Gehrig solidly entrenched at first base for the Yanks, he would have a difficult time seeing playing time unless he moved to another position. So Greenberg signed with the Tigers and became a major star.

Before he did, however, he had to overcome a few obstacles, such as his lack of coordination and insidious religious prejudice from opponents almost as vicious as what Jackie Robinson would endure more than a decade later.

After three solid years in the minor leagues, Greenberg was called up to the Tigers in 1933, batted .301, hit 12 home runs, and drove in 87 runs in 117 games. The following year, he batted .339, hit 26 homers and a league-leading 63 doubles, drove in 139 runs, and helped the Tigers win their first pennant in 25 years. He followed that up by leading the league in home runs with 36 and RBI with 170 in 1935 and being named AL Most Valuable Player. But a broken wrist sustained in Game 2 of the World Series sent him to the sidelines, where he watched the Tigers win their first world championship.

Greenberg came back in 1936 and had 16 RBI and a .348 average in 12 games when he broke the same wrist again in a collision at first base. Not only was he out for the season, but there also was wide speculation that his career was over.

Greenberg put those rumors to rest the following season by hitting a robust .337 with 40 homers and an incredible 183 RBI (in only 154 games), the third-highest total in baseball history.

The following year, Greenberg made his bid at passing Babe Ruth's illustrious single-season home run record of 60. With five games to play, he had 58 home runs, tied with Jimmie Foxx for the most home runs by a right-handed hitter and two away from Ruth's cherished mark. But Greenberg could not add to his total. Ruth's record, which had stood for 11 years and would stand for another 23 until Roger Maris broke it in 1961, remained untouched.

Over the next two seasons, Greenberg continued to put up big numbers. In 1940, he moved from first base to left field to accommodate young slugger Rudy York and batted .340, led the league with 41 homers and 150 RBI, became the first player to win MVP awards at two different positions, and led the Tigers to another pennant.

With hostilities heating up in Europe, Greenberg was drafted into the service 19 games into the 1941 season. A congressional edict that released men over age 28 from the military enabled Greenberg to get an honorable discharge on December 5, 1941. Two days later, the Japanese bombed Pearl Harbor, setting off America's involvement in World War II, and Greenberg volunteered for service in the U.S. Air Force. He attended Officers Candidate School, was commissioned a first lieutenant, and served in the China-Burma-India Theater scouting locations for B-29 bases.

Greenberg would miss all of 1942, 1943, and 1944 and return for 78 games in 1945. A salary dispute prompted the Tigers to sell Greenberg's contract to the Pittsburgh Pirates in 1947. At first reluctant to move to another team in a different league, Greenberg ultimately agreed to play his final season under a contract that, with incentives, made him the National League's first $100,000 player.

In Pittsburgh, Greenberg befriended and mentored a young home run hitter named Ralph Kiner. To take advantage of their twin right-handed sluggers, 24-year-old Kiner and 36-year-old Greenberg, the Pirates moved their bullpen in front of Forbes Field's cavernous left-field wall, creating an inviting target that fans dubbed "Greenberg Gardens." The Pirates' two sluggers combined for 76 home runs, 51 for Kiner and 25 for Greenberg.

As an indication of the magnitude of Greenberg's career, here it is more than 60 years since he played his last game for the Tigers, and he still owns the franchise's top three single-season slugging percentages, the top four seasons in total bases and RBI, and the top season for doubles and home runs.

On the franchise's all-time career list, Greenberg is ninth in total bases, eighth in batting average and doubles, sixth in RBI, and first in slugging percentage. Al Kaline has the most home runs by a Tiger: 399. Greenberg is third with 306. But Kaline had 11,597 plate appearances; Greenberg had 5,586.

If the numbers he put up in 1961 had been the norm, not the exception, we would be talking here about Norman Dalton Cash, Hall of Famer—and not just **Norm Cash**, the No. 2 first baseman in Tigers history.

In that magical year of '61, Cash led the American League in batting with an average of .361, 37 points better than the runner-up, his teammate and

Norm Cash had his best batting year in 1961. Unfortunately, the nation's attention was on the "M&M Boys," Yankees sluggers Roger Maris and Mickey Mantle, and their race to break Babe Ruth's single-season home-run record.

roommate Al Kaline (Cash never batted higher than .286 in any of his other 16 seasons and had a lifetime average of .271) and in hits with 193 (he never had more than 168 in any other season). He hit 41 home runs (the only time he topped 40) and drove in 132 runs (he never drove in more than 93 in any other season).

Despite those glittering statistics, Cash was only sixth in the American League in home runs, fourth in RBI, and fourth in the Most Valuable Player voting.

That was the year of the storied and controversial home-run race, the chase for Babe Ruth's record of 60 home runs in a season by the M&M Boys, Roger Maris and Mickey Mantle. It was "the year of the asterisk," so called because Ruth had hit his 60 in a 154-game season and that year, 1961, the American League had expanded the schedule to 162 games.

Maris would break the record with 61 homers, lead the league in RBI with 142, and win the Most Valuable Player award. Even on his own team, Cash was overshadowed by Rocky Colavito, who outhomered Cash, 45 to 41, and led the team in RBI with 140, eight more than Cash.

There was no hint or even the slightest thought of players using steroids back then—so how do you explain a guy hitting 90 points above his career average and driving in 39 more runs than he did in any other season?

One explanation is that in 1961 the American League had expanded from eight teams to 10 and, consequently, pitching was diluted. Another is something I heard right from the horse's mouth, Cash himself. While I was with the Tigers, Norm spent a few years as a color analyst on the Tigers' cable telecasts. One day, I was in the clubhouse for some reason and the game was on. The announcers were talking about the great year Norm had in 1961. I heard Cash comment that he used a corked bat the entire year. I couldn't believe my ears. I remember thinking, "Why in the world would anybody admit to that?" Whether he was joking or serious, I don't know, but he said it over the air and later he said it to *Sports Illustrated*—even going so far as to demonstrate how he drilled a hole in his bat and filled it with sawdust, cork, and glue.

I couldn't believe he would say a thing like that over the air. But that was Norm. Another time I was in the clubhouse getting a cup of coffee, and I heard the announcers describe a ball hit into the stands and a scramble for the ball by a bunch of fans. Cash said, "Baseball is the only sport that you can see somebody completely ruin a $60 pair of slacks trying to get a $5 baseball."

*F*ew men enjoyed their time as a major league baseball player as much as Norm Cash, one of the game's blithe spirits and natural wits. His self-depreciating and sardonic humor is legendary in the annals of Tigers baseball.

"When you mention Norm Cash, I just smile," said Al Kaline, who roomed with Cash and lockered next to him. "He was a fun guy to be around and a great teammate."

On July 15, 1973, in Tiger Stadium, Nolan Ryan, pitching for the California Angels, was one out away from the second no-hitter of his career. He had struck out 17 when he faced Cash, who had struck out twice and grounded out to second base.

When Cash stepped into the batter's box, he was toting not a baseball bat but a table leg he had taken from the clubhouse.

"You can't use that," said home-plate umpire Ron Luciano.

"Why not?" Cash inquired. "I won't hit him anyway."

Cash acceded to Luciano's command and exchanged the table leg for a regular baseball bat, with which he popped to short to end the game.

One time Cash was hung up, darting between first and second base, about to be tagged out, when he stopped dead in his tracks and formed a "T" with his hands to call time out.

Another time, he chased a foul ball to the stands near first base where a young boy was seated, eating popcorn. Cash reached in for the ball and was unable to grab it. Before returning to his position, he took the boy's baseball cap off his head, turned it around, reached into the popcorn box, grabbed a handful of popcorn, and said, "Thanks, kid."

His teammate Jim Northrup remembered another antic Cash occasionally pulled. If Cash was on base and there was a rain delay, when the game resumed, according to Northrup, "If Norman was on second before the rain delay, he would go to third; if he was on first, he would go to second."

Cash once summed up his major league career as follows: "I owe my success to expansion pitching, a short right-field fence, and my hollow bats," a reference to his admission that, when he won the American League batting championship in 1961, he used a corked bat.

Norm was a Texan who had been an outstanding college football player, good enough, in fact, to be drafted by the Chicago Bears as a running back. He turned down the Bears and signed a baseball contract with the White Sox. Cash wasn't getting much of a chance to play and was included in a big seven-player deal between the White Sox and Indians. He never even got into a game with the Indians before he was traded again, this time to the Tigers for third baseman Steve Demeter. It was one of the best trades the Tigers ever made. Demeter played only four games for the Indians and batted five times without a hit, while Cash played 15 years for the Tigers and had 1,793 hits.

Every time I talked with some of the older-generation Tigers who were around before I got there, they all referred to Cash as a fun-loving character and a great guy to have on the team, someone who kept everybody loose all the time. Apparently Norm was one of those guys that would, on occasion, stay out all night. I remember one of the trainers telling me that Cash would come in the next morning, looking like death warmed over, and grab a bottle of Pepto-Bismol off the counter, gulp the whole bottle down, and then go out and play the game.

Norm was kind of a cutup, but there obviously was a lot of love for him from his teammates. Bill Freehan always had some stories to tell about him. I never appreciated how good a player Cash was until recently when I started doing some research. He had an outstanding career and was one of the most productive players in the American League at his position in the decade of the 1960s.

One of the better defensive first basemen in his day, Cash led the league in putouts once, fielding percentage twice, and assists three times. He's No. 1 on the Tigers' all-time list of first basemen in games played, putouts, assists, and double plays.

But it was his offensive consistency that set Cash apart from the run-of-the-mill first basemen. The year after he led the league in batting, Cash's average fell to .243. The 118-point decline is the largest ever for a batting champion. By way of explanation, Cash said the reason for the drop in his average was that the Tigers were paying him to hit home runs.

And hit home runs he did, 30 or more in five seasons during an era when 30 home runs were a lot and often enough to lead the league. He hit 20 or more 11 times, including nine years in a row. He finished his career second to Kaline on the Tigers' all-time home run list, third in the American League in home runs as a first baseman, and fourth in the AL (behind Babe Ruth, Lou Gehrig, and Ted Williams) in home runs by a left-handed batter. In 1961, he became the first Tiger to hit a ball over the right-field roof in Tiger Stadium and did it three more times after that.

Norm also set a few quirky baseball records, which is no surprise to the people who knew him best.

- In a game against Minnesota, he had no chances at first base.
- In the 1960 season, in more than 400 plate appearances, he did not hit into a double play.
- He had two hits in one inning in Game 6 of the 1968 World Series.

Sadly, Cash suffered a tragic and untimely death in 1986 when, at the age of 51, he slipped while on a boat in Lake Michigan, struck his head, fell in the water, and drowned.

Rudy York was born to be a designated hitter—which is to say he was born too early, some 60 years before the American League adopted the DH rule. By the time York retired as an active player, the designated hitter was still some 25 years in the future, and when he died, it was three years before the DH rule was enacted.

The Tigers never could find a position for York, but one thing he could always do was hit.

A powerfully built man at 6'1" and 210 pounds, York hit more than 30 home runs for the Tigers four times and drove in more than 100 runs five times. He had been discovered playing baseball for the textile mill in which he worked as a teenager and was signed by the Tigers in 1933. After being named Most Valuable Player as a first baseman for Beaumont in the Texas League in 1935 and for Milwaukee in the American Association in 1936, he was promoted to Detroit only to find that patrolling first base was none other than Hank Greenberg, like York, a right-handed hitter with enormous power.

The Tigers tried York at third base and in left field and found him a defensive liability at both positions. When player/manager Mickey Cochrane sustained a career-ending beaning, York was handed a catcher's mitt and became the Tigers' regular catcher for the final third of the season. As a catcher, York was equally inept, but the Tigers could not ignore the rookie's potent bat.

Rudy York's deficiencies on the field were sufficiently overshadowed by his power at the plate.

On the final day of August, York hit two home runs, which gave him 18 for the month and surpassed Babe Ruth's record of 17 homers in the month of September 1927. York also broke the record for most RBIs in a month with 49. He would finish his rookie season with a .307 batting average, 35 homers, and 103 RBI in only 375 at-bats.

York continued to pile up impressive offensive numbers while also frustrating the Tigers with his defensive deficiencies. Finally, in 1940, the Tigers found a resolution to their problem. They decided that York would do the team the most good, and cause the least harm, at first base. To entice Greenberg into giving up his preferred position, they offered him a bonus if he would move to left field. Greenberg accepted.

The move was a bonanza for the Tigers. Batting back to back in the lineup, Greenberg and York were the scourges of the American League, combining for 74 home runs (Greenberg led the league with 41; York was third with 33) and 284 RBI (Greenberg led the league with 150; York was second with 134).

The Tigers, who had won 81 games the previous year and finished in fifth place and 26½ games behind the Yankees, won 90 games in 1940 and finished in first place by a game over Cleveland.

York would be the Tigers' first baseman and continue to put up strong offensive numbers for the remainder of his days in Detroit. In 1943, with many big stars, including Greenberg, in military service during World War II, York, who at 33 was beyond draft age, led the American League with 34 home runs and 118 RBI. Although he became an adequate defensive first baseman, York never dazzled anyone with his glove. As one sportswriter said of York, who was one-eighth Cherokee Indian, "Rudy York is part Indian and part first baseman."

After the 1945 season, York was traded to the Red Sox, with whom he had a brief resurgence. He teamed up with Ted Williams to form a one-two punch netting 55 homers (38 for Williams, 17 for York) and 242 RBI (123 for Williams, 119 for York) leading the Red Sox to their first pennant in 28 years. In the World Series against the Cardinals, York hit two home runs and drove in five.

But it was in Detroit that York had his best years. His 239 home runs as a Tiger ranks seventh on the team's all-time list, and his slugging percentage of .503 is fourth behind Hall of Famers Hank Greenberg, Harry Heilmann, and Ty Cobb.

Cecil Fielder had to travel halfway around the world to find his stroke and become the prodigious power hitter most baseball people thought he would be when he was drafted by the Kansas City Royals in the fourth round of the June 1982 draft.

Less than eight months after they drafted him, the Royals traded Fielder to the Toronto Blue Jays. After three seasons in the minor leagues, he arrived in Toronto in 1985. Still, he failed to make any kind of impact and was relegated to being a backup and occasional right-handed replacement for two left-handed power hitters, Willie Upshaw and Fred McGriff.

In four seasons, Fielder would appear in only 220 games for the Blue Jays and only 65 at first base (he was used as a designated hitter 127 times, played seven games at third base, one in left field, and even got in two games at second base), with only 31 home runs and 84 RBI.

Cecil Fielder was at the
peak of his batting
powers during his six
years in Detroit.

After the 1988 season, Fielder received an offer he could not refuse from the Hansin Tigers of the Japan Central League. Hansin was offering a one-year contract for $1.05 million, plus a chauffeur and a full-time interpreter. It was a no-brainer for Fielder, who had earned $125,000 in Toronto.

More than the money, it was an opportunity for Fielder to play full time, and he made the most of it by belting 38 home runs, which caught the attention of the Detroit Tigers. They signed him as a free agent for $1.25 million and brought him back to the United States in 1990 to be their first baseman.

At that point, Fielder's career took off like a rocket. When he got to Detroit, he lit up the stadium. On the last day of the '90 season in Yankee Stadium, he hit two home runs, his 50th and 51st of the year, making him the 11th player in baseball history, the first in 13 years, and the first Tiger in 52 years to hit at least 50 homers.

He would lead the American League in home runs in 1990 and '91 and in RBI in 1990, 1991, and 1992. He was named to the American League All-Star team in 1990, '91, and '93. Every time I think of Fielder, what's the first thing that comes to my mind? Home runs! In his six years in Detroit, he had four consecutive 30–home run–100-RBI seasons. He's the only Tiger to have hit at least 25 home runs for six straight seasons and one of four players (the others were Harmon Killebrew, Frank Howard, and Mark McGwire) to have hit a ball over the left-field roof at Tiger Stadium.

Cecil wasn't a great first baseman, but he did the job. He moved around pretty well and was surprisingly graceful and agile for a big man, 6'3" and upward of 260 pounds. I don't believe he did himself any favors by letting his weight to balloon like it did, but for those five or six years, he was as feared and dangerous a power hitter as there was in baseball.

The way he started out, **Tony Clark** looked as if he was going to be one of the great players in Tigers history, right up there with the Greenbergs, Gehringers, and Kalines. I always thought he had that kind of potential. He was big and strong, a switch-hitter with power who could really hit the ball. And he was very graceful, agile, and sure-handed at first base.

In his first three full seasons, Clark hit 97 home runs and drove in 319 runs. Unfortunately, the next year he was injured, missed more than 100 games, and was never the same after that.

Tony was a baseball and basketball star in college, at the University of Arizona and San Diego State. At 6'7", he probably could have had a career in the NBA, but when the Tigers made him the second pick in the country in the June 1990 free-agent draft, the bonus money apparently was too inviting for him to pass up.

I honestly don't know what happened to Tony after those first few years. It might have been the injuries, and it might have been something else. When you're a good player and you get on a good team, things just seem to fall into place, and you just keep going and going. But when you're a good player and you get on a team that's struggling, they expect you to do more than you may be able to do.

In the seven years he was in Detroit, the Tigers never had a winning season. For most of that time, Clark was pretty much their only offensive

At 6'7", Tony Clark was a big presence on the field. He was also the biggest contributor to the Tigers' offense during the lean years in the late '90s.

threat. He was a big, imposing figure of a man, a great guy, very likeable, very intelligent, never a problem. But he wasn't outspoken, and the Tigers felt they needed a leader, somebody to take charge of the team, and they targeted Tony to be that guy. The role just didn't fit his personality.

That was the one knock against him. He seemed content going through his career the way he decided he wanted to go through it. People tried to light a fire under him to get him more motivated because they felt that's what he needed. But Tony was Tony. That wasn't his nature, and so he simply faded away. They eventually moved him and got somebody else.

Tony didn't stick around long enough to notch his place in Tigers history, but he has moved around to a bunch of clubs. He's had a nice, long career and has played on a couple of division champions.

When I began compiling my all-time Tigers team, Miguel Cabrera had recently arrived in Detroit in a trade with the Florida Marlins and, in fact, had just started playing first base after five years as a third baseman in Florida.

Because of his limited time with the Tigers, it was premature to include him among my top five first basemen, but based on what he has accomplished in such a short time, I have no doubt that Cabrera will move up rapidly on the list of all-time Tigers first basemen.

It would be asking too much to expect him to vault over Hank Greenberg to the top of the list, but it is not too far-fetched to expect that, in another year or two, Cabrera will be considered the second-best first baseman in Tigers history.

Statistical Summaries

All statistics are for player's Tigers career only.

HITTING

G = Games

H = Hits

HR = Home runs

RBI = Runs batted in

SB = Stolen bases

BA = Batting average

First Baseman	Years	G	H	HR	RBI	SB	BA
Hank Greenberg *Homered in four consecutive at-bats over two games on July 26 and 27, 1938*	1930, 33–41, 45–46	1,269	1,528	306	1,202	58	.319
Norm Cash *Had three pinch-hit homers in 1960*	1960–74	2,018	1,793	373	1,087	42	.272
Rudy York *Played 150 or more games for eight consecutive seasons from 1940–47*	1934, 37–45	1,268	1,317	239	936	34	.282

continued	Years	G	H	HR	RBI	SB	BA
Cecil Fielder *Led AL in total bases with 339 in 1990*	1990–96	982	947	245	758	2	.258
Tony Clark *Broke Bill Walton's San Diego high school basketball season scoring record in 1990*	1995–2001	772	783	156	514	6	.277

FIELDING

PO = Putouts

A = Assists

E = Errors

DP = Double plays

TC/G = Total chances divided by games played

FA = Fielding average

First Baseman	PO	A	E	DP	TC/G	FA
Hank Greenberg	9,581	645	95	888	10.1	.991
Norm Cash	14,926	1,303	127	1,328	8.6	.992
Rudy York	8,628	735	106	1,079	10.0	.989
Cecil Fielder	6,280	604	61	619	9.3	.991
Tony Clark	5,967	452	50	601	9.5	.992

THREE

Second Baseman

With all he accomplished on the field and how he conducted himself on the field and off, there is no more popular, honored, revered, and admired Tiger than **Charlie Gehringer**.

As a man he was humble, soft-spoken, classy, dignified, gentlemanly, and loyal.

As a baseball player he was durable, dependable, and consistent. In 1969, he was named baseball's greatest living second baseman by a special committee of baseball writers.

To add to his popularity among Tigers fans, Gehringer was a true son of Michigan, a homegrown hero born on a farm in Fowlersville, Michigan, a small town about 100 miles northwest of Detroit. He spent a year at the University of Michigan, played his entire 19-year major league career with the Tigers and lived out his latter years in the Detroit suburb of Bloomfield Hills.

1.	CHARLIE GEHRINGER
2.	LOU WHITAKER
3.	PLACIDO POLANCO
4.	DICK McAULIFFE
5.	EDDIE MAYO

It was in the fall of 1923, just after he had completed his freshman year at college, that Gehringer was discovered by Tigers outfielder Bobby Veach, a pretty fair country hitter himself and, like Gehringer, a left-handed batter.

A top 10 fixture in most offensive categories, Charlie Gehringer remains one of the Tigers' most beloved players.

Veach arranged for the youngster to spend a week working out at Navin Field under Tigers supervision. Player/manager Ty Cobb, another pretty good lefty, was sufficiently impressed with young Gehringer to advise owner Frank Navin to sign the kid.

Gehringer started his professional career with London in the Class B Michigan-Ontario League in 1924 and was called up late that season to play in five games for the Tigers. He spent the 1925 season with Toronto of the International League and again got a late call-up with the Tigers for eight games. He finally reached Detroit to stay in 1926 and took over the second base job from veteran Frank O'Rourke.

By 1927, Gehringer was a star, batting .317—the first of five straight years over .300. His consistency at bat and in the field prompted Yankees pitcher Lefty Gomez to dub Gehringer "the Mechanical Man."

Teammate Doc Cramer said of Gehringer, "You wind him up on Opening Day and forget him."

And Mickey Cochrane, who would manage Gehringer from 1934–38, said, "Charlie says hello on Opening Day, goodbye on Closing Day, and in between hits .350."

Sometimes he even hit higher than .350: like in 1934 when he batted .356, 1936 when he batted .354, and 1937 when he led the American League with a .371 average, 20 points higher than Lou Gehrig and 25 points higher than Joe DiMaggio.

Never having seen him, I can't tell you much about Gehringer's defense, but he is said to have been slick and sure-handed. You can tell a good deal about a hitter by his statistics in comparison to others of his day, but defensive statistics often don't give a true picture of a player's fielding skills. Nonetheless, it should be mentioned that Gehringer led American League second basemen in fielding percentage nine times, led or tied for the league lead in assists seven times, and led in putouts three times.

Still, it's his offense that stands out and that undoubtedly got him elected to the Hall of Fame with 85 percent of the vote in 1949: a .320 lifetime batting average, 2,839 hits, 184 home runs, 1,427 RBI, and 182 stolen bases. He had more than 200 hits seven times, led the league in hits twice, had more than 100 RBI seven times, was the American League's Most Valuable Player in 1937 and finished in the top 10 in MVP voting for seven straight years. He started and played every inning of the first six All-Star Games.

As an indication of his versatility, Gehringer also led the league in doubles twice, triples once, and stolen bases once.

On the all-time Tigers list, Gehringer is seventh in batting average; second in runs scored and doubles; third in at-bats, hits, total bases, triples, bases on balls, and extra-base hits; fourth in games played and RBI; fifth in on-base percentage; and ninth in stolen bases.

Another little-known attribute of Gehringer was his unflagging devotion to his mother, a diabetic. When his father passed away in 1924, Gehringer dedicated himself to caring for his mother and didn't marry until after his mother passed away.

When he wed, in 1949, Gehringer was 46 years old, and even then he showed his loyalty and his dignity. He was elected to the Hall of Fame that year but chose not to attend the induction ceremony in Cooperstown because it was scheduled for June 13, and he did not want it to interfere with his wedding, which took place five days later.

Longevity and consistency are the hallmarks of **Lou Whitaker**'s outstanding career. He was another guy who played his entire major league career with the Tigers, all 19 seasons of it. In that time, he batted below .263 only three times, drove in fewer than 42 runs only once, and had a stretch of 11 straight years and 13 out of 14 with home runs in the double digits.

Lou Whitaker was amazing. The Tigers signed him as a third baseman but moved him to second base to pair him with shortstop Alan Trammell. Their thinking was, *We can have ourselves something here in these two young guys for a long time if Whitaker can get the hang of playing second base.* Well, he certainly did get the hang of it, and the Tigers got more than even they could have hoped for—a double-play duo that played together longer than any other pair in history, 19 seasons.

Whitaker put in a lot of hard work, and he took to second base like he had been playing the position since Little League. He had an exceptionally strong arm for a second baseman. I've never seen a second baseman who could go behind second base, backhand the ball, turn around, and throw to first base with as much accuracy and as much on the ball as Lou put on it. He had excellent hands, and he and Trammell turned the double play as well as anyone I've ever seen.

And Lou could flat out hit. He had tremendous power for a guy his size, which was about 5'11", 160 pounds in his prime. Early in his career, he didn't hit a lot of home runs, but after a while he realized he could reach those seats and what the formula was to hit the long ball. If you laid something out over the plate, he could turn on it and drive it a long way. He went on a streak, reaching double figures in home runs, and in 1989 he hit 28 out of the park. He's also on the list of guys who have hit the ball over the Tiger Stadium roof.

Whitaker was just a pure hitter. Spring training would start and all of the hitters would be behind the pitchers until they had a little batting practice to warm them up. In games, nobody could touch the pitcher at the beginning because every batter's timing was off. Lou never had a problem with that. It was amazing to me that he could come to spring training, without picking up a bat all winter long, step in the cage the first day, and spray line drives all over the place. He looked like he was in midseason form.

I remember one time we were taking batting practice and Lou got upset with somebody for some reason—I can't remember who or why—but Lou

Lou Whitaker was the very model of consistency.

just decided he wasn't going to take batting practice any longer. He didn't take BP for about a month, but when the games started, he turned it up a notch and hit the cover off the ball. He was phenomenal in that regard. It was like he was a plug-in hitter—just stick him in the batter's box, plug him in, and he's good to go.

Whitaker had a great career. I still marvel at one play he made in Game 1 of the 1984 World Series against San Diego. It was the bottom of the seventh and we were leading 3–2. Kurt Bevacqua, who killed us all Series long, led off with a shot into the right-field corner, into the bullpen. Kirk Gibson was chasing it down, and he had to get under the benches in the bullpen to get the ball.

Not only do their 19 seasons as shortstop and second baseman for the Detroit Tigers make Alan Trammell and Lou Whitaker the longest-running double-play combination in baseball history, it also makes them No. 1 on another, more exclusive list.

MOST YEARS TOGETHER AS TEAMMATES

19—Alan Trammell and Lou Whitaker, Detroit, 1977–95

18—Fred Clarke and Honus Wagner, Louisville, 1897–99; Pittsburgh 1900–11; 1913–15*

18—Joe Judge and Sam Rice, Washington, 1915–32

18—George Brett and Frank White, Kansas City, 1973–90

* Before the Louisville team went out of business in 1900, the victim of underfinancing, Clarke and Wagner were traded to Pittsburgh. Suffering with leg problems, Clarke retired in 1912 but returned to appear in nine games in 1913, two in 1914, and one in 1915.

MOST YEARS TOGETHER AS DOUBLE-PLAY PARTNERS

19—Alan Trammell and Lou Whitaker, Detroit (AL), 1977–95

12—Shawon Dunston and Ryne Sandberg, Chicago (NL), 1985–95, 1997

12—Joe Tinker and Johnny Evers, Chicago (NL), 1902–13

10—Billy Rogell and Charlie Gehringer, Detroit (AL), 1930–39

8—Dave Concepcion and Joe Morgan, Cincinnati (NL),1972–79

7—Luke Appling and Jackie Hayes, Chicago (AL), 1932–38

7—Billy Jurges and Billy Herman, Chicago (NL), 1932–38

7—Luis Aparicio and Nellie Fox, Chicago (AL), 1956–62

7—Dick Groat and Bill Mazeroski, Pittsburgh (NL), 1956–62

6—Jack Barry and Eddie Collins, Philadelphia (AL), 1909–14

6—Frank Crosetti and Tony Lazzeri, New York (AL), 1932–37

6—Chico Carrasquel and Nellie Fox, Chicago (AL), 1950–55.

6—Tony Kukek and Bobby Richardson, New York (AL), 1959–61, 1963–65

6—Ozzie Smith and Tommy Herr, St. Louis (NL), 1983–88

6—Cal Ripken Jr., and Billy Ripken, Baltimore (AL), 1987–92

Baseball wisdom dictates that you never make the first out or the last out of an inning at third base, but Bevacqua, obviously thinking he had an easy triple, went tearing around second base, heading for third, as Gibby was trying to dig the ball out from under the bench. He came up with it and fired a strike to Whitaker, who had gone down into short right field to position himself properly as the cutoff. Lou got the throw from Gibson, turned around and threw a strike, right on the bag, to third baseman Marty Castillo, who tagged Bevacqua trying to stretch a double into a triple.

That play to me typified Lou Whitaker, his baseball savvy, arm strength, and accuracy. He got that relay throw, turned around, and fired a pea to third base, right on the bag, and all Castillo had to do was drop his glove on the bag and Bevacqua, the tying run, slid right into the tag.

It was a big play for us because it erased the tying run—they would not get another hit off Jack Morris, who went the distance for the win—and it was a statement-making play for Lou Whitaker.

When his career was over, Whitaker had put up some very impressive and consistent numbers over many seasons. He was the 1978 American League Rookie of the Year; a five-time AL All-Star, three times as a starter; won three Gold Gloves and four Silver Sluggers; and had a lifetime batting average of .276, with 2,369 hits, 244 home runs, and 1,084 RBI.

On the Tigers' all-time lists, he's in the top 10 in games, at-bats, runs, hits, total bases, doubles, home runs, runs batted in, walks, and stolen bases and in the top six in all of those categories except RBI and stolen bases.

The first time I saw **Placido Polanco** was in the late 1990s when I managed San Antonio in the Dodgers' farm system; Polanco was playing for Little Rock. He was just working his way through the Cardinals' farm system, and he caught my eye. I tabbed him as a good fielder who swung the bat extremely well, a good contact guy.

When you manage or coach in the minor leagues, one job requirement is to file daily reports on not only your own players but also on every opponent. I remember giving Polanco high marks on all facets of the game. I didn't see him too many times, but I saw him enough that I said in my reports that *This guy's a prospect; he's got good tools, good hands, and a good bat.* You never know how a young player will turn out because there are so many variables and

Placido Polanco's hitting and defense galvanized the Tigers in the first part of the 21ˢᵗ century.

intangibles that determine one's success, but Polanco turned out to be a much better hitter than I ever thought he would be.

Fast forward to 2004. Alan Trammell had been named the Tigers' manager, and he asked me to be one of his coaches. When we got there in '03, the Tigers were about as rock-bottom as a team could get, so we were trying to get anybody we could who might help our cause. We signed Pudge Rodriguez as a free agent, and he kept trying to convince the Tigers to sign Ugueth Urbina. Pudge had known Ugie when they played together with the Marlins.

Urbina was a hard thrower who had saved 32 games the previous season. He was a free agent, but nobody would sign him. We would soon find out why. Pudge kept vouching for him, saying what a great guy he was and all that, and we badly needed help in the bullpen so the Tigers signed Urbina on Rodriguez's recommendation.

It wasn't too long before Urbina wore out his welcome in Detroit. He saved some games, but he seemed to blow almost as many as he saved. He wasn't much help, as we still lost 90 games. Besides that, he was something of a problem in the clubhouse, so Ugie wasn't winning any friends in Detroit. Fans, sports talk show hosts, the writers, and even some players were urging the Tigers to get rid of him. Finally, midway in the 2005 season, general manager Dave Dombrowski, who had been trying without success to trade Urbina, made a deal with the Phillies: Urbina for Placido Polanco.

I understood that the Phillies needed help in the bullpen, and they wanted to play Chase Utley at second base, but getting Polanco was like pulling a rabbit out of a hat. We were trying to unload Urbina, and Dombrowski was looking to get a body in return—and he got Polanco, who turned out to be just an unbelievable player.

From the day he arrived in Detroit, Polanco has been nothing but impressive in my eyes. He is like a hitting machine. And he plays great second base. He puts all these streaks together—consecutive games without making an error, getting on base, games with no strikeouts—and he's a great guy. I'm thinking, *Dave Dombrowski's got the Midas touch.*

Polanco had some pretty good years before he got to Detroit—a .316 average in 2000 and a .307 average in '01 with the Cardinals—but it seemed as if teams were always looking to replace him with somebody better. When he came to the Tigers, Placido really blossomed. He batted .338 in '05 and was third in the league in '07 with a .341 average.

What really impressed everyone about him was his baseball intelligence—how he did the little, intangible things to win games—and his outstanding character. In three straight years, '06–'08, he led the American League in at bats-per-strikeout ratio. In 2007 he broke the major league record for consecutive errorless games and consecutive errorless chances by a second baseman and became the first everyday second baseman in history to play an entire season without committing an error.

Polanco was a Tiger only five years when he was traded back to Philadelphia, but despite his short tenure in Detroit, Placido did enough in my mind to rate ahead of every Tigers second baseman except Charlie Gehringer and Lou Whitaker.

I came to the Tigers in 1977, right on the heels of the 1968 World Series championship team. Dick Tracewski, who played on that '68 team, was a coach with the Tigers when I got there. So was Gates Brown, who also played on the '68 team. So naturally, I heard a lot about the guys on that championship team. **Dick McAuliffe** was one name that came up frequently, and although I can't remember ever meeting him, I feel like I know him from all the complimentary things I heard about him.

They said that he was a very important part of that championship team, a tough, hard-nosed player who was the team's leadoff man and offensive catalyst. He led the American League in runs scored, drew 82 walks, hit 16 home runs, drove in 56 runs, had 50 extra-base hits, an on-base percentage of .344, and was seventh in the American League MVP voting. In the World Series

A steady second baseman, Dick McAuliffe was a key component of the 1968 World Series–winning team.

victory over the Cardinals, he had six hits, scored five runs, hit a home run, and drove in three runs.

McAuliffe was originally signed as a shortstop, and that was his primary position until 1967, when he was shifted to second base. That first year, he made 21 errors at second. But he obviously worked hard and reduced that number to nine errors in the championship season.

People who saw him play will invariably bring up his unusual batting stance. A left-handed hitter, he held his hands high above his head, and he had an open stance, with his right foot pulled so far to the right it appeared as if he was practically facing the pitcher. But he had a lot of power for a guy his size: 5'11", 175 pounds. He reached double figures in home runs for 10 straight seasons, hit more than 20 three times, drove in more than 50 runs nine times, and hit .260 or better six times.

In 16 big-league seasons, 14 of them with the Tigers, McAuliffe hit 231 doubles, 71 triples, and 197 home runs.

Eddie Mayo doesn't get the credit he deserves because most of his major league career came during World War II, when many of the game's best players were in military service. But it should be pointed out that Mayo had one of his best years in 1947, after the war was over and all the great stars had returned. At age 37, he played in 142 games, batted .279 (27 points above his career average), hit six home runs, drove in 48 runs, and, with only 12 errors in more than 700 chances, had a fielding percentage of .983.

Edward Joseph Mayoski, the son of Polish immigrants, was born in Holyoke, Massachusetts, and raised in Clifton, New Jersey. He signed with the Tigers in 1932. After four minor league seasons, he was traded to the New York Giants in 1936 and played in 46 games as a backup third baseman. In three years, he would appear in 119 games, mostly as a backup player, before spending five seasons with the Los Angeles Angels of the Pacific Coast League, where he drew the attention of major league scouts.

With so many players in military service, Mayo got a second chance in 1943 when the Philadelphia Athletics drafted him and made him their starting third baseman. For the first time in his major league career, Mayo was a regular.

But an eye injury affected his hitting, and he slumped to .219 with only 28 RBI. Surprisingly, the eye injury didn't affect his fielding; he led the league's third basemen in fielding percentage.

45

A star while many major leaguers were "over there," Eddie Mayo actually had his best year in 1947, two years after the War. *Courtesy of AP Images*

Citing his poor eyesight, the Athletics released Mayo, but the Tigers took a chance and claimed him in the Rule 5 draft. Back with the team with which he originally signed gave new life to Mayo, who was given a chance to start over. The Tigers asked him to switch to second base, a position he had never played in 247 major league games.

The change proved to be a blessing for Mayo, who fielded his new position at an excellent percentage of .978 and led American League second basemen with 120 double plays. His hitting also improved by 30 points to .249, and he showed some latent power with 18 doubles and 63 RBI.

In the following year, Mayo raised his batting average to .285 and had career highs of 24 doubles and 10 home runs. He teamed with fellow 35-year-old Skeeter Webb, a shortstop, to form a double-play combination that led the Tigers to the American League pennant.

In the deciding seventh game of the World Series against the Chicago Cubs, Mayo had two hits and scored two runs in the 9–3 victory that nailed down the championship.

In balloting for the American League 1945 Most Valuable Player award, Mayo finished second to teammate Hal Newhouser, who paid the Tigers' second baseman a great tribute, calling him the "take-charge guy in our infield."

Statistical Summaries

All statistics are for player's Tigers career only.

HITTING

G = Games

H = Hits

HR = Home runs

RBI = Runs batted in

SB = Stolen bases

BA = Batting average

Second Baseman	Years	G	H	HR	RBI	SB	BA
Charlie Gehringer *Played in team-record 511 consecutive games between 1927–31*	1924–42	2,323	2,839	184	1,427	181	.320
Lou Whitaker *Homered to lead off two consecutive games vs. Angels in 1983*	1977–95	2,390	2,369	244	1,084	143	.276
Placido Polanco *Hit .529 to win MVP of 2006 American League Championship Series vs. Oakland*	2005–09	632	806	37	285	26	.311

continued	Years	G	H	HR	RBI	SB	BA
Dick McAuliffe *Went the entire 1968 season without grounding into a double play*	1960–73	1,656	1,530	192	672	61	.249
Eddie Mayo *Led league with 28 sacrifices in 1944*	1944–48	587	586	23	229	26	.265

FIELDING

PO = Putouts

A = Assists

E = Errors

DP = Double plays

TC/G = Total chances divided by games played

FA = Fielding average

Second Baseman	PO	A	E	DP	TC/G	FA
Charlie Gehringer	5,369	7,008	309	1,444	5.8	.976
Lou Whitaker	4,771	6,653	189	1,527	5.0	.984
Placido Polanco	1,318	1,775	19	463	5.0	.994
Dick McAuliffe	2,032	2,184	97	519	4.7	.978
Eddie Mayo	1,334	1,564	65	367	5.4	.978

FOUR

Shortstop

It has been said that timing is everything in life, but it sure hasn't been everything good for **Alan Trammell**, who came along in baseball at the wrong time. Put him in almost any other era, and Tram would be hailed as one of the game's great shortstops and probably would have been elected to the Hall of Fame by now. His misfortune was that he was overshadowed as a shortstop by some of the game's magical names.

Trammell's career spanned 20 seasons, from 1977 until 1996. And look at who else was playing shortstop in the majors at that time. You can start (and probably end) with Cal Ripken Jr. and Ozzie Smith—both in the Hall of Fame, both perennial All-Star starters (Ozzie started for the National League every year from 1983–92; Cal was the starting American League shortstop every year from 1984–96).

1. ALAN TRAMMELL

2. HARVEY KUENN

3. CARLOS GUILLEN

4. BILLY ROGELL

5. ED BRINKMAN

Other shortstops in that period were Dave Concepcion, Garry Templeton, Larry Bowa, and Barry Larkin in the National League; Robin Yount, Tony Fernandez, Ozzie Guillen, and Bert Campaneris in the American League.

And just as Trammell's career was winding down, along came Alex Rodriguez, Derek Jeter, and Nomar Garciaparra.

Trammell doesn't have the career stats to compare with some of those guys. He wasn't an Iron Man like Cal Ripken or a big home run/RBI guy like Ripken, Yount, and A-Rod. He didn't play in a big-media city like Jeter or Garciaparra. But for my money, I'd put him up there with any of those shortstops.

Tram didn't have a lot of flair, glitz, or flash; he was the polar opposite of Ozzie Smith. But fundamentally, he was as sound as anybody you could run out there. He always got himself in the proper position, made all the plays, and made them look easy. He was very intelligent and positioned himself so well that it seemed like the ball was always hit right to him. He didn't have the strongest arm, but I don't recall him ever having a problem throwing the ball to first base. He always hit the first baseman right in the chest.

Tram was practically robotic: catch the ball, make the little crow hop, get in the right position, put something on the throw, and get it right on the money.

As a hitter, he was clutch and a tough out. We used to call him "the Fiddler" because he had the knack of "fiddling" the ball in for a hit better than anybody. He never tried to do too much. He would spray the ball around. When he had two strikes on him, he was as good as anybody at just putting the ball in play; he got quite a few hits doing that. Guys would marvel at his ability to flare one over second base. He could "doink" one into right field or center field with the best of them, and that's how he got his nickname.

Don't get me wrong, Trammell could hit. I wouldn't consider him a power hitter, but on occasion he could produce the long ball when you least expected it. In Game 4 of the 1984 World Series, for example, he hit a pair of two-run home runs in his first two at bats off Eric Show, and we beat the Padres 4–2 to take a 3–1 lead in the Series.

Another time we were in Kansas City and trailing in the seventh inning. The Royals brought in their closer, Dan Quisenberry, a submariner known for getting ground balls. Of all the things you would never expect to happen, Tram beat Quiz with a grand slam. Later Quisenberry, who had a great sense of humor, told the reporters, "That's the longest ground ball I ever served up."

One of the things about Tram that stands out in my mind—and I wasn't even there to see it—was the year he had as a hitter in 1987. I had been the

A good shortstop among a field of exceptional shortstops, Alan Trammell doesn't get the credit he deserves for his accomplishments.

Tigers' cleanup hitter for the previous few years, but then I left Detroit to sign with Philadelphia as a free agent and the Tigers didn't really have a cleanup hitter. Sparky Anderson moved Trammell in the four hole, and Tram responded with the best year of his career, a .343 average, third in the league, with 205 hits, 28 home runs, and 105 RBI—all career highs. He was asked to be the team's run producer, and he did it.

I didn't know his exact numbers that year; I had to look them up. But Tram wouldn't have had to. He would have known them off the top of his head: not only his statistics but the statistics of other players. Trammell is a sports junkie. And not just baseball, any sport. Baseball, football, basketball, hockey—he follows them all.

I've never known anybody who was as into sports as Trammell. Usually, professional athletes are not big sports fans because they were too busy playing sports to follow them closely when they were growing up. But Tram is the consummate sports fanatic. He knows everything about everything and everybody. I'm sure that's true to this day. I think he knows every college basketball team in existence, their nicknames, their colors, who coaches them, who plays for them, when they won this, when they won that. It's unbelievable.

He's a big Lakers fan, he follows football, and he knows everything there is to know about baseball. He reads every issue of *Baseball America, The Sporting News*, and S*ports Illustrated* from cover to cover. He keeps reading them until the next one comes out, so he memorizes everything about everybody. If you were to put a TV in front of him, he would turn it on only for a sporting event—he has no interest in watching anything else.

I'll take a page from Trammell now and give you some of his career numbers, such as seven seasons with a batting average of .300 or better, six All-Star Game selections, and four Gold Gloves. He was the runner-up in the 1987 American League Most Valuable Player voting, and he's in the top 10 on the all-time Tigers lists in games played, at-bats, runs, hits, total bases, doubles, RBI, bases on balls, and stolen bases.

Unfortunately, after having such a brilliant career in Detroit, Tram went back and sullied his reputation when he took the job as manager. In three years, he won 186 games and lost 300, a percentage of .383. But you can't blame all that on Tram, who had never managed before.

At the time, the Tigers were at the lowest point in their history. They had gone nine straight years without a winning record. In the previous eight years, they had won 526 games and lost 750, a percentage of .412 and an average of 93.8 losses a year. There was little hope of Trammell, or anybody else, being able to turn things around right away, and I believe the Tigers knew that and that they hired Tram because he was such a popular player in Detroit.

Eventually, Trammell had to be sacrificed and was fired. He didn't win, but what he accomplished in those three years was to change the culture in the clubhouse and further the development and acceleration of young players such as Curtis Granderson, Placido Polanco, Marcus Thames, Craig Monroe, Brandon Inge, Jeremy Bonderman, and Nate Robertson, who would be key players in the Tigers' 2006 American League championship a year after Tram's dismissal.

Early in the 1950s, the Tigers signed two young free agents who would have a strong impact on Detroit Tigers baseball for the next two decades: an 18-year-old high school outfielder from Baltimore named Al Kaline and a 21-year-old shortstop from the University of Wisconsin–Madison named **Harvey Kuenn**.

Both of these precocious young players would be playing in the big leagues within months after signing. When Kaline, without ever spending one day in the minor leagues, joined the Tigers in June 1953, Kuenn was already installed as the team's regular shortstop, having come up to the Tigers for 19 games after playing only 63 games in the low minor leagues.

By 1954, both youngsters were Tigers mainstays, Kuenn the shortstop and leadoff batter, Kaline batting sixth and playing right field.

In his first two full seasons, Kuenn led the American League in hits with 209 in 1953 and 201 in 1954. In his first four seasons, he batted .308, .306, .306, and .332, accumulating 796 hits.

Kuenn was the Tigers' regular shortstop for his first five seasons and made the All-Star team every year, and in 1955–57, he was the American League's starting shortstop. In 1958, the Tigers shifted him to the outfield. He was their center fielder in 1958 and then played mostly right field in 1959, when he had 198 hits and won the batting championship with a .353 average.

Two days before the Tigers were to open the 1960 season in Cleveland, the Tigers and Indians brokered one of the most shocking and controversial trades in baseball history. The Tigers sent the defending American League batting champion Kuenn to Cleveland in exchange for Rocky Colavito, who

Detroit's 1960 trade of Harvey Kuenn to Cleveland in exchange for Rocky Colavito sent shock waves through the baseball world. It remains the only time in history that the defending batting champion has been traded for the top home-run hitter.

had hit 42 home runs in 1959 and tied with Harmon Killebrew for the American League home run crown. It was the first and only time in baseball history that a defending batting champion was traded for a defending home-run king.

Although he batted .308 for the Indians and out-hit Colavito by 59 points, Kuenn was never accepted in Cleveland, where Colavito had been immensely popular. The Indians fans seemed to prefer Rocky's home runs to Kuenn's high average, and Kuenn hit only nine homers that year while Colavito belted 35 in Detroit.

After one season in Cleveland, Kuenn was traded again. He went to San Francisco and resumed what was an outstanding career, finishing with a lifetime batting average of .303.

When his playing career was over, Kuenn returned home to Wisconsin and became a coach with the Milwaukee Brewers. In June 1982 he took over as manager and wound up winning the American League pennant with an outstanding hitting team that was nothing like its manager. They were a bunch of bombers, including Ted Simmons, Cecil Cooper, Robin Yount, Paul Molitor, Ben Oglivie, Gorman Thomas, and Don Money—collectively nicknamed "Harvey's Wallbangers."

I was a coach with the Tigers in 2004 when they acquired **Carlos Guillen** from the Seattle Mariners for Ramon Santiago, another great trade made by general manager Dave Dombrowski. Guillen became a star for the Tigers, and a few years later the Tigers got Santiago back. Dave Dombrowski's a wizard. I don't know how he does it.

For pure talent, you won't find too many guys who are better than Guillen. If there's one negative thing about him, it's about his body. He just hasn't been able to stay healthy. Something is always wrong—from tuberculosis in 2001, to a torn ACL in 2004, to problems with his hamstring in 2005. If he could have stayed healthy, there's no telling what kind of numbers he could have right now.

When he has been healthy, Carlos has put up some impressive numbers—such as 2004, his first year with the Tigers, when he batted .318, hit 20 homers, and drove in 97 runs; or 2006, when he batted .320, hit 19 homers, and drove in 85; or 2007, when he batted .296, hit 21 homers, and drove in 102.

In 2006, Guillen became the 10th Tiger to hit for the cycle and the first player in the modern era to increase his batting average in six consecutive seasons.

I became a big fan of Guillen when he came over to Detroit. I would watch him take ground balls, and he was like a machine: a great fielder with great hands. On his own, he would take hundreds of ground balls every day. Nobody had to go get him. He was always out there ready to take ground balls. He would take 50, 60 at a time and make the turn to second base on his double-play throw. He would consistently work all angles of the field, backhanding balls, going up the middle—he did it all.

What I liked most about him was the way he interacted with the younger players. They all looked up to him. Whenever we'd get a young Hispanic infielder, Carlos would take him under his wing, and he'd be out there with the young guy, showing him the ropes, telling him what he needed to work on. He did that with quite a few young guys. As a player, Carlos was a coach's dream: a great guy with a great work ethic who was great in the clubhouse. He's the whole package.

As good as his career has been, it could have been even better if he had been able to stay on the field. He still might end up with a Hall of Fame career (you never know), but his body has been fighting him on that, which is unfortunate.

Injury problems have hampered what has otherwise been a stellar career for Carlos Guillen.

It took **Billy Rogell** seven years to land a starting job in the major leagues, but once he got his foot in the door he refused to let go.

Longevity and durability were Rogell's forte. He spent eight seasons as the Tigers' regular shortstop.

He joined with second baseman Charlie Gehringer to form a longstanding double-play pairing that played together for more than 1,000 games, a Tigers record that lasted until it was surpassed by Alan Trammell and Lou Whitaker four decades later.

When his playing days were over, Rogell served 36 years as a member of the Detroit City Council, playing a key role on the city's planning commission (the road entering Detroit's Metropolitan Airport is William G. Rogell Drive) and coming to the aid of indigent former baseball players residing in the Detroit area.

At age 94, he threw out the first ball for the final game at old Tiger Stadium. He died in 2003, three months before his 99th birthday.

Rogell was originally signed by the Boston Red Sox and struggled for four years before he was released. Playing for St. Paul in the American Association, Rogell caught the eye of major league scouts by batting .336 and driving in 90 runs. He sifted through several offers before accepting Detroit's.

At first, he was no more successful in Detroit than he was in Boston, but given a chance to play every day late in the 1931 season, Rogell batted .303 in 48 games and began the 1932 season as the Tigers' starting shortstop. From that point on, his career flourished.

With Rogell, a switch-hitter, installed as their leadoff man and the glue of their infield, the Tigers became an American League power, improving from back-to-back fifth-place finishes in 1932–33 to back-to-back pennants in 1934–35.

In 1934, Rogell led off in front of future Hall of Famers Mickey Cochrane (their player/manager), Charlie Gehringer, Hank Greenberg, and Goose Goslin; batted .296; scored 114 runs; and drove in 100 runs. The infield of Greenberg, Gehringer, Rogell, and Marv Owen combined to drive in 462 runs, a major league record.

In addition to being their offensive catalyst and spark plug, Rogell gave the Tigers aggressive and superb defense and leadership. He led American League shortstops in fielding for three straight years from 1935–37 and in assists for two straight years, 1934–35.

A stellar defenseman, Billy Rogell is perhaps best remembered for an unfortunate play: hitting baserunner Dizzy Dean during the 1934 World Series. *Courtesy of AP Images*

In the 1934 World Series against the Cardinals, Rogell had eight hits and four RBIs despite playing with a broken ankle. However, he is probably best remembered for a play he made in the field. It came in Game 4 when pitcher Dizzy Dean was inserted as a pinch runner for Spud Davis, who had singled in a run in the fourth inning. The next batter, Pepper Martin, hit a ground ball to second baseman Gehringer, who fired to Rogell to force Dean. Rogell's relay throw to first hit Dean on the forehead and ricocheted into the outfield about 100 feet away.

The unflappable Dean was taken to the hospital for precautionary X-rays. Later, Ol' Diz would reveal the result of the examination. "The doctors X-rayed my head and found nothing," he said.

Don't be misled by the offensive numbers: .224 batting average, 60 home runs, and 461 RBI for more than 6,000 at bats, averaging to four homers and 30.7 RBI per season. You don't get to play 15 years in the big leagues—10 of those years as a regular shortstop with at least 132 games—for such demanding

Numbers don't tell the whole story for Ed Brinkman. He was an indispensable man on the roster during his four-season stint in Detroit. *Courtesy of AP Images*

managers as Gil Hodges, Ted Williams, Ralph Houk, and Billy Martin (who had him in three different places) if you can't help their teams.

Ed Brinkman could and did help every team he played with because of his outstanding defense and his ability and willingness to do the little things that help a team win.

I loved Eddie Brinkman. When I came into the Tigers organization, Brinkman was installed as a coach, scout, and instructor. He was such a fun guy to be around. I guarantee that if you mention Eddie Brinkman's name to everyone who knew him, you would put a smile on their faces. He was just fun, a happy-go-lucky guy who was full of crazy baseball stories and had a distinctive, funny little laugh.

Eddie came from Cincinnati, where he was a high school teammate of Pete Rose. He liked to tell people that he was a better player in high school than Rose, and that was no doubt true because Pete got $7,000 to sign with the Reds and Eddie got $75,000 to sign with the Washington Senators. Brinkman once said, "Pete always kidded me that the Washington Senators brought me my bonus in an armored truck, and he cashed his check at the corner store."

Eddie wasn't a superstar. He was a solid player who did a great job for you defensively but wasn't going to help you a whole lot offensively. No matter. I've known managers like Gene Mauch who, if you could play an important position like shortstop and do a good job defensively, he didn't care what you hit. He just wanted you to catch the ball, make the plays, and he'd get his offense somewhere else. Eddie Brinkman was one of those guys.

In 1972, when the Tigers finished first in the American League East, Brinkman won the Gold Glove, had an errorless streak of 72 games and 331 chances, was voted "Tiger of the Year" by the Detroit baseball writers, and finished ninth in the Most Valuable Player voting despite batting only .203.

Statistical Summaries

All statistics are for player's Tigers career only.

HITTING

G = Games

H = Hits

HR = Home runs

RBI = Runs batted in

SB = Stolen bases

BA = Batting average

Shortstop	Years	G	H	HR	RBI	SB	BA
Alan Trammell *Batted .419 with 3 homers and 9 RBI in 8 postseason games in 1984*	1977–96	2,293	2,365	185	1,003	236	.285
Harvey Kuenn *Led league in at-bats each of his first two seasons (1953–54)*	1952–59	1,049	1,372	53	423	51	.314
Carlos Guillen *.412 career batting average with bases loaded*	2004–09	721	801	86	402	57	.301

continued	Years	G	H	HR	RBI	SB	BA
Billy Rogell *Walked in record 7 straight plate appearances in 1938*	1930–39	1,207	1,210	39	532	76	.274
Ed Brinkman *Hit one of Tigers' 4 home runs in first inning at Cleveland, 6/29/74*	1971–74	630	458	28	180	3	.222

FIELDING

PO = Putouts

A = Assists

E = Errors

DP = Double plays

TC/G = Total chances divided by games played

FA = Fielding average

Shortstop	PO	A	E	DP	TC/G	FA
Alan Trammell	3,391	6,172	227	1,307	4.6	.977
Harvey Kuenn	1,343	2,114	129	430	4.8	.964
Carlos Guillen	642	1,423	76	301	4.4	.965
Billy Rogell	2,245	3,700	265	772	5.4	.957
Ed Brinkman	954	1,981	67	349	4.8	.978

FIVE

Third Baseman

So sue me because I'm picking **Travis Fryman** over George Kell as the No. 1 third baseman on my all-time Tigers team.

Yes, I know Kell made the Hall of Fame and Fryman didn't. And I know that Kell had a lifetime batting average of .306, 32 points higher than Fryman's. I would never take anything away from Kell, who had a great career and was a dear friend, but this is the *Tigers* all-time team, remember, and a good part of the statistics Kell compiled, he did with four other teams.

What's more, when it comes to power numbers, there's no comparison. Fryman hit 223 homers, 149 with the Tigers, to Kell's 78, 25 of them with the Tigers. Fryman drove in 1,022 runs, 679 with the Tigers, to Kell's 870 and 414 with the Tigers.

1.	TRAVIS FRYMAN
2.	GEORGE KELL
3.	RAY BOONE
4.	PINKY HIGGINS
5.	TOM BROOKENS

That's why Fryman gets my vote as the No. 1 third baseman in Tigers history.

Fryman was the Tigers' first-round pick, No. 30 in the country, out of Lexington, Kentucky, in the June 1987 free-agent draft. It was the year after I left Detroit, so I never played with him. I did meet him, spent some time

Travis Fryman provided some offensive snap on some of the anemic Detroit Tigers teams of the 1990s.

with him, played against him, and watched him play. What stood out about him was his businesslike approach to the game. Where some guys like to joke around and have some fun, Travis was very serious.

Playing against him and watching him play on television solidified my opinion that he was a very good player. He had good pop, he hit home runs, he drove in runs, and he was solid at third base. With the Tigers, he hit 20 or more home runs five times, and drove in more than 90 runs five times and more than 100 twice. I'd say that's pretty good production.

One thing that worked against him is that in Detroit, he didn't play on very good teams. In the 10 years Fryman was there, the Tigers finished with a winning record only twice. But they were a big offensive club with some pretty good bangers, such as Mickey Tettleton, Cecil Fielder, Rob Deer, Lloyd Moseby, Pete Incaviglia, and Eric Davis. Trammell and Whitaker were still there—and then Fryman came along, and so did Kirk Gibson, followed by Bobby Higginson and Tony Clark.

For a few years, if you were an American League pitcher, you did not want to face the Detroit Tigers because they could just pound you. But they couldn't hold anybody down, either. The Tigers of the 1990s were a team that could rake and could score some runs, and Travis Fryman was a big force in that offense.

If he had played his entire 15-year career with the Tigers, I would have had no choice but to bury my admitted prejudice in favor of run production guys over high average guys and picked **George Kell** as the No. 1 third baseman in Tigers history.

The fact is, Kell played only parts of seven seasons with the Tigers. Although he batted over .300 in every full season with them, he drove in more than 59 runs just twice (whereas Travis Fryman drove in 81 runs or more seven times) and never reached double figures in home runs (Fryman hit at least 15 home runs seven times).

So I'm putting Kell at No. 2 among Tigers third basemen, and I'm doing so regrettably because George is one of my favorites. I never saw him play, but I have studied his career stats, talked with many who did see him play, and got to know George quite well. He was a legend in Detroit as a Tigers broadcaster for 37 years, including my entire tenure with the Tigers.

Kell was from Arkansas, and I will always remember his Southern drawl coming through in his broadcasts. Early in my career, the TV station put together a reel of my highlights, and George narrated it. In all the years I was there, I don't remember him saying one bad thing about anyone on the air. He was very gracious in the booth and off the air. He was a great guy who was always very complimentary and very cordial.

As a player, people tell me he was regarded as the American League's best third baseman in the 1940s and early 1950s. He was a 10-time All-Star, led the league in fielding percentage seven times, in assists four times, and in chances once. He batted over .300 nine times, had a lifetime .306 average, and, in his Tigers years, had averages of .327, .320, .304, .343, .340, .319, and .296.

His .343 came in 1949 and was Kell's only batting title. Ted Williams, seeking his third straight batting title, had led the league throughout most of the season. Going into the final day, Williams held a three-point edge on

Beloved by Detroit fans, longtime radio broadcaster George Kell was also a solid Tigers third baseman.

Kell, .344 to .341. But while Williams was hitless in two official at-bats at Yankee Stadium, Kell, playing at home against Cleveland, had two hits in three trips to finish at .34291 to Williams' .34275, thereby depriving Williams—who would lead the league in home runs and tie for the lead in RBI—of a third triple crown and a third straight batting title.

One could say that **Ray Boone** is the patriarch of baseball's "first family": the first family with three generations of major leaguers—and all of them All-Stars—Ray, his son Bob, and Bob's sons Bret and Aaron.

There have been other families with three generations of big leaguers—the Bells, the Hairstons, and the Schofield/Werths—but the Boones got there first, on August 19, 1992, when Bret Boone broke in with the Seattle Mariners, 32 years and eight days after his grandfather, Ray, played his final major league game.

Bret Boone's granddad, Ray, broke in with Cleveland in 1948 as a short-stop and showed some promise with the bat in his early days: a .301 average, seven home runs, and 58 RBI in 109 games in 1950. The Tigers, meanwhile, were in the throes of a horrendous stretch and in dire need of offensive punch. In 1952, they won only 50 games and finished dead last in the eight-team American League. In an attempt to remedy the problem, on June 15, 1953, the Tigers and Indians completed an eight-player trade that brought Boone to Detroit.

[Ed. note: By coincidence, Lance Parrish was a member of the Seattle Mariners when Bret Boone made his major league debut playing against Baltimore. Parrish was the designated hitter and batted cleanup. He had a double in four at-bats in Seattle's 10–8 victory. Boone played second base and batted seventh and singled in a run in his first major league at-bat.]

The Tigers had a promising 22-year-old rookie shortstop named Harvey Kuenn, so the plan was for Boone to move to third base, a position he had played in only two games for the Indians in four years. The switch paid immediate dividends as Boone reached career highs in batting average at .312, home runs with 22, and RBI with 93 in only 101 games after the trade.

Over the next few years, Boone would become one of the most produc-tive third basemen in the American League. He was voted the starting third baseman in the 1954 All-Star Game and hit a home run off Robin Roberts.

The following year, Boone and Jackie Jensen of the Red Sox tied for the American League lead in RBI with 116, eight ahead of Yogi Berra. A series of injuries to his knees and ankles limited Boone's range, and in 1957 he moved across the diamond to first base. A year later, on June 15, he was traded to the White Sox in a deal that brought Terry Francona's dad, Tito, to the Tigers.

In five-plus seasons, Boone batted .291 for the Tigers, hit 105 home runs, and drove in 460 runs.

Through the years I have had a connection with the Boone family in one way or another, including being a teammate of Bret's when I played in Seattle in 1992 and he was just a kid breaking into the big leagues. My relationship with Bob, Bret's dad, is even more coincidental. I didn't play on a single team with Bob, but I seemed to follow in his footsteps and even came close to being his teammate once. I joined the Phillies six years after Bob left, and in 1989, after he left the California Angels and signed as a free agent with Kansas City, I was traded from the Phillies to the Angels and became Bob's replacement.

Ray Boone was the first of three generations of major league ballplayers.

I had long admired him for his longevity and his skill as a catcher. We became good friends, living fairly close to each other in Southern California and both under contract to Nike. Every off-season, Nike put together a trip for the All-Star players who wore their shoes. They called us their advisory board, and our purpose was to discuss ideas for improving the product, though it was really more of a social occasion. We went to Hawaii, Las Vegas, and places like that for a week, and we could bring a guest, your wife or your significant other, a relative or friend.

On those trips, I got to meet and become good friends with a lot of guys, including Mike Schmidt, Steve Carlton, Wade Boggs, Kirk Gibson, Gary Carter, Ryne Sandberg, Carlton Fisk, and Bob Boone. Boone brought his wife on those trips and I brought my wife, Arlyne, and our two wives spent time together and became the best of friends.

Speaking of coincidences, my brother-in-law, Marc Leventhal, to this day tells me that Ray Boone was his favorite player growing up. Marc wasn't a fan of the Tigers or the Indians, and he wasn't from Detroit or Cleveland. He was just a baseball fan. Why and how he ever latched on to Ray Boone, I have no idea.

I also remember Marc telling me that when my son David was playing college ball, his University of Michigan team took a West Coast trip and was playing in San Diego, and Arlyne, her sister Cheryl, and he went to watch the game. Who should be there but Ray Boone, who was from San Diego. Bob Boone wasn't there, but Bob's wife, Sue, was and Marc asked her to introduce him to his favorite player.

Sue Boone made the introductions, and Marc and Ray talked for a while. Ray told Marc a story about the first time he and Ted Williams were on the same field together. Williams also was from San Diego, and on this day, Williams and Boone each had about three or four hits. Ray was playing third base, and on Williams' last at-bat, he hit one in the gap, circled the bases, and slid into third with a triple. According to Ray, up to that time he had never spoken a word to Williams. Now Williams had slid into third base with a triple, got up, dusted himself off, looked over at Ray with a grin, and said, "It looks like they can't get anybody out from Herbert Hoover High School today."

It turned out that not only were Williams and Boone both from San Diego, but Williams also knew that they had gone to the same high school five years apart.

For five years from 1933–37, Marv Owen held down third base for a Tigers team that won two American League pennants, one World Series, and finished second twice.

A competent if unspectacular defender, Owen was a solid contributor to a team that boasted such powerful batters as Hall of Famers Hank Greenberg, Mickey Cochrane, Charlie Gehringer, Goose Goslin, and Al Simmons. In that five-year span, Owen batted .286 and drove in 382 runs.

In 1934, Owen helped the Tigers end a 25-year pennant drought when he batted a career-high .317 and drove in 96 runs, joining with first baseman Greenberg, second baseman Gehringer, and shortstop Billy Rogell to form one of the best-hitting infields in baseball history. The four combined for 769 hits, 462 RBI, and 179 doubles. Three of the four batted over .300 (Gehringer .356, Greenberg .339, Owen .317) and the fourth member, Rogell, batted .296. Rogell, Gehringer, and Owen played in all 154 games. Greenberg played in 153.

Yet for all his offensive production and his huge contribution to the Tigers' success, Owen is best remembered as the centerpiece and trigger for one of the most memorable and controversial plays in World Series history.

It came in Detroit's Tiger Stadium in the sixth inning of the climactic seventh game of the 1934 World Series between the Tigers and St. Louis Cardinals. The Cards had broken the game open with seven runs in the third inning and were coasting to their third World Series title in nine years behind their brilliant and colorful 30-game winner, Dizzy Dean.

The Cardinals increased their lead to 8–0 when Pepper Martin led off the top of the sixth with a single and scored after two outs when the redoubtable and swashbuckling Joe "Ducky" Medwick, who would tie Detroit's Gehringer for the highest average of the Series with a .379 mark, rattled a triple off the bleachers in right-center field.

Medwick raced full tilt around the bases and slid hard into third base—*A little too hard, considering the score*, thought Tigers third baseman Owen. The two scuffled briefly in the dirt before being separated by umpires.

When the inning ended and Medwick took his place in left field, he was pelted by a barrage of garbage—bottles, fruit, and vegetables—tossed onto the field by the frustrated Tigers fans. Three times Medwick left his position and returned to the cover of the Cardinals dugout, but each time he returned to the field, the barrage continued. Finally, baseball commissioner Kenesaw Mountain Landis, sitting in a field level box, summoned both managers, Mickey Cochrane of Detroit and Frankie Frisch of St. Louis, along with the umpires, and ordered Medwick removed from the game, "for his own safety."

After a delay of 20 minutes, the game resumed. The Cardinals tacked on two more runs in the seventh and Dean completed the shutout, allowing six hits and striking out six as the Cardinals completed an 11–0 victory and a baseball championship.

The disappointed Tigers fans got their chance to celebrate a year later when the Tigers won their second-straight pennant and beat the Chicago Cubs in the World Series in six games, the clincher coming in Tiger Stadium.

In 1936 Detroit slipped to second place in the American League, 19½ games behind the New York Yankees, who were led by Lou Gehrig and a spectacular rookie named Joe DiMaggio.

Marv Owen held up his end for the '36 Tigers, batting .295 and driving in 105 runs, the sort of numbers that today would be worth a king's ransom. Instead, 14 months later, Owen was traded to the Chicago White Sox as part of a six-man deal.

Pinky Higgins was already a six-year major league veteran with the Philadelphia Athletics and Boston Red Sox when the Tigers acquired him in a trade with Boston after the 1938 season. The hope was that Higgins would plug the Tigers' gaping hole at third base that had existed first when Marv Owen's production fell off dramatically and then after he was traded.

Although he didn't match the offensive production of his days with the Athletics (a batting average that ranged between a high of .330 and a low of .289, 64 home runs, and 363 RBI in four seasons) or his two years in Boston (batting averages of .302 and .303 and 106 RBI each season), Higgins provided the Tigers with excellent defense, veteran leadership, and adequate and consistent production at bat.

In six full seasons in Detroit, Higgins' batting average ranged from a high of .298 to a low of .267, his home-run output from a high of 13 to a low of seven, and his RBI from a high of 84 to a low of 73.

Though better known for his days in Boston as a player and manager, Pinky Higgins (left, with Cincinnati's Billy Werber) was a consistent contributor during his four years in Detroit.

After finishing first or second for four straight seasons, the Tigers slipped to fourth place in 1938. There was no immediate improvement when Higgins came aboard, but in his second year he helped the team win another pennant and then batted .333 in the 1940 World Series.

Higgins remained consistent over the next four years, but the Tigers would not reach the World Series again until 1945, when Higgins was in military service. He returned in 1946 and on May 19 was sold to the Red Sox, with whom he would have a long association as player, manager, and general manager.

Tom Brookens never made the All-Star team. In 10 seasons with the Tigers, he never batted higher than .275, never stole more than 14 bases, never hit more than 13 home runs, or drove in more than 66 runs. In short, he wasn't a big power guy, which teams look for from a power position like third base.

What Tommy Brookens was, however, was a winner and a gamer—and an All-Star in my book. He is a guy you want playing for your team.

The best way to describe Brookens is that he was a scrappy player. He'd get in the dirt with anybody, and he'd get the job done. He had a great work ethic, and he was a very talented guy who did his job. He also had a great sense of humor. He was the life of the team, a great personality, a lot of fun. Everybody loved Brookie.

Just about every year, it seemed, somebody would come along who was going to take his third-base job away from him, but when push came to shove, there was Brookens right back where he always was.

Brookens and I broke into the Tigers organization together. In the minor leagues, he was a shortstop/second baseman, but with Alan Trammell and Lou Whitaker ahead of him, it was obvious he was not going to play short or second in the big leagues. The Tigers converted him into a third baseman, he worked hard at learning the position, and he became a very good one. At the same time, he was always available to play wherever the Tigers needed him. He was a guy you could throw in to play anywhere on the field in a pinch.

This will tell you a lot about Brookie's versatility: In his major league career, he played 1,065 games at third base. But he also played 162 games at second, 119 games at shortstop, 23 as a DH, six in right field, two in center

Brookie was the very definition of a utility player.

field, two at first base, and even one as a catcher (how he missed playing in left field and pitching, I'll never know).

I'll never forget the game he caught. It was in Detroit against the Texas Rangers. I was out with an injury, so Bob Melvin got the start at catcher and we were playing one of those marathon games where manager Sparky Anderson had to make all kinds of moves. Late in the game, he took Melvin out for a pinch-hitter and put Marty Castillo in to catch.

At one point, we were losing and Castillo was due up. With a chance to tie the score late in the game, Sparky wanted to use a pinch-hitter for Castillo, but he was out of catchers. That's when he got this brainstorm. Turning to Brookens, he said, "Hey, I need a catcher. Can you catch?" Brookie said, "Yeah, put me out there."

Now get this picture. I'm 6'3" and 220 pounds and Brookens is 5'10", 170, and he's wearing my catching gear. The shin guards were too big, and the chest protector made him look as if he was wearing body armor. He looked so out of place. But he went back there and did the job for five innings and we won the game in the fifteenth.

One day we were playing in Cleveland, and Tommy was having a rough day. He struck out for the third or fourth time, and as he was coming back to the dugout, he was about two or three feet away when he dropped to the ground and rolled into the dugout. I mean he literally rolled into the dugout, hit the floor, and kept rolling under the bench where he lay for a minute or two. Even Sparky had to laugh.

Another time, in Texas, we had a Ranger hung up between third and home. I had the ball, ran him back to third, and lunged to tag him before he got to the bag. As I did, I did sort of a cartwheel and went flying to the ground, head over teakettle. As I tumbled, I collided with Brookie, and my spike went right through his upper lip.

Brookie's blood was all over the ground, and they sent for an ambulance, carted him away to a hospital where they stitched him up, and sent him back. In those days, Tommy had a big, bushy mustache. To stitch up his lip, they had to shave part of it—so when he came back from the hospital, he had half a mustache.

The next day Brookie's lip was swollen to twice its normal size, but gamer that he was, he played anyway. It wasn't funny at the time, but it is now when I think of him coming to bat with that big, bushy mustache on one side of his upper lip and this swollen, stitched-up balloon on the other side.

Statistical Summaries

All statistics are for player's Tigers career only.

HITTING

G = Games

H = Hits

HR = Home runs

RBI = Runs batted in

SB = Stolen bases

BA = Batting average

Third Baseman	Years	G	H	HR	RBI	SB	BA
Travis Fryman *Led league in sacrifice flies in 1994 with 13*	1990–97	1,096	1,176	149	679	58	.274
George Kell *Went 6-for-7 at Cleveland on 9/20/46*	1946–52	826	1,075	25	414	34	.325
Ray Boone *Hit his first two major league homers in consecutive innings at Boston on 6/15/49*	1953–58	683	723	105	460	8	.291

continued	Years	G	H	HR	RBI	SB	BA
Pinky Higgins *Collected hits in record 12 consecutive at-bats for Boston during 1938 season*	1939–44, 46	857	878	60	472	25	.280
Tom Brookens *Singled in first major league at-bat on 7/10/79*	1979–88	1,206	871	66	397	85	.246

FIELDING

PO = Putouts

A = Assists

E = Errors

DP = Double plays

TC/G = Total chances divided by games played

FA = Fielding average

Third Baseman	PO	A	E	DP	TC/G	FA
Travis Fryman	534	1,549	74	136	2.8	.966
George Kell	933	1,663	78	156	2.9	.971
Ray Boone	572	1,050	71	110	3.4	.958
Pinky Higgins	874	1,616	171	121	3.2	.936
Tom Brookens	702	1,712	143	163	2.6	.944

SIX

Left Fielder

A glance at the major league record of **Bobby Veach** reveals the numbers of a man who deserves serious consideration for the Hall of Fame—a lifetime batting average of .310 in 14 major league seasons, 12 of them with the Tigers; 64 home runs in what was the "dead-ball" era, 1,166 RBI, more than Hall of Famers Lou Brock, Chick Hafey, and Ralph Kiner; nine seasons with a batting average above .300; six seasons with more than 100 RBI; three times the American League RBI leader; two seasons with more than 200 hits.

And yet, despite such an impressive resume, in all the years he was eligible, Veach received just one vote for the Hall of Fame. One! It came in 1937, the second year of Hall of Fame voting when Napoleon Lajoie, Tris Speaker, and Cy Young were elected. Seventy-one players received more votes than Veach.

1. BOBBY VEACH

2. WILLIE HORTON

3. ROCKY COLAVITO

4. GOOSE GOSLIN

5. HEINIE MANUSH

How to account for such a glaring oversight? One explanation is that Veach spent his entire career in the shadow of, and in the same outfield with, some of the game's greatest players. All 12 of his Detroit years were spent as a teammate of three Hall of Fame players who combined to win 16 batting

Despite posting numbers that rivaled those of his better-known contemporaries such as Babe Ruth, Tris Speaker, and teammate Ty Cobb Bob Veach was never inducted to the National Baseball Hall of Fame.

titles, the incomparable Ty Cobb, Harry Heilmann, and "Wahoo" Sam Crawford.

The mention of Tris Speaker's name brings up an interesting comparison. While the illustrious "Grey Eagle" is regarded as one of the greatest pure hitters baseball has known (his lifetime batting average of .345 is sixth all-time) and his 22-year career gives him a decided edge in numbers over Veach, who played 14 seasons, Veach more than holds his own with Speaker in head-to-head competition.

In the 14 years they were contemporaries, Speaker had the higher batting average 13 times. However, Veach hit more home runs than Speaker seven times and drove in more runs nine times.

Veach's best season was 1919, when he batted .355, second in the league to Cobb; drove in 101 runs, second in the league to Babe Ruth; tied with Cobb for the league lead in hits; and led the league in doubles with 45, seven more than Speaker, and in triples with 17, two more than Heilmann. A year later, he became the first Tiger to hit for the cycle when he got six hits in a 12-inning game.

Perhaps the best indication of how good a hitter Veach was is to examine his eight most productive years, from 1915 to 1922. In that span, Veach had 852 RBI and 450 extra-base hits, more than Cobb, Ruth, Speaker, and George Sisler.

In 1925, the final year of his career, Veach split time between the Washington Senators and New York Yankees and earned the distinction of being the only player to ever pinch-hit for the mighty Babe Ruth after the Bambino had switched from pitcher to the outfield.

81

When you talk about **Willie Horton**, you're talking about one of the all-time fan favorites in the history of the Tigers. He's from the area, he played sandlot ball and high school ball in Detroit, and he was part of the 1968 team that won the World Series. Add to that his role during the Detroit street riots in 1967 when, wearing his Tigers uniform, he stood on a car in the middle of the unruly and angry mob and pleaded for calm. Later he walked through the neighborhoods and tried to do whatever he could to ease the tension and put an end to the riots. He went the extra mile to try to get things under control and back in order. The city owes him a large debt of gratitude for his efforts.

Willie Horton is one of the six Tigers players enshrined at Comerica Park.

All of these things combine to make him a beloved figure in Detroit and the embodiment of the Detroit Tigers at the time.

Overlooking Comerica Park from the left field concourse are six larger-than-life statues of Tigers legends Ty Cobb, Hank Greenberg, Charlie Gehringer, Al Kaline, Hal Newhouser, and Willie Horton.

Horton may not have had a Hall of Fame career, the numbers of a super-star, or the kid of production you might expect from a traditional power position like left field. In 12 full seasons with the Tigers, he batted over .300 twice. I never heard anyone say he was a great defensive outfielder, primarily because of his lack of speed, but he had good hands and he made a great throw to nail Lou Brock attempting to score in Game 5 of the 1968 World Series.

Willie Horton's persona transcends his baseball career, however. His statue is a tribute not so much to his baseball career but an honor to him for all he has done for the city.

Willie was born in a small town in Virginia, the youngest of 21 children. When you grow up the youngest of 21 kids, you learn to fight for everything you get, and Willie was a fighter. The family moved to Detroit when Willie was very young. He led Detroit's Northwestern High School to the city baseball championship and was a legend in Detroit when he was just a teenager. I heard stories from people who saw him play as a kid about the prodigious home runs he would blast into oblivion and what a great player he was.

When I first came up, Horton was still playing. In spring training, most of the players stayed at a Holiday Inn in Lakeland around Lake Parker that was a few miles down the road from the ballpark where we trained and played exhibition games. I can't tell you how many times I was driving to the yard on the road that went along the edge of the lake and I'd see Horton, dressed in Army boots and full Army fatigues over a rubber suit, jogging to the ballpark. Willie was constantly working to control his weight. He stood 5'11" and could weigh anywhere from 210 to 240 or more.

He was an imposing physical figure. Guys told me that when the Tigers got into team fights, players on the other team would always keep their eyes on Willie. They wanted to know where Willie was, because when he got that look in his eyes, nobody wanted to go near him. He would go ballistic and take on anybody who came close to him.

For someone who played only four years as a Tiger, **Rocky Colavito** sure made his mark in Detroit. I got to Detroit almost 20 years after he had played there, but if someone mentioned the name Rocky Colavito, the reaction was always the same, "The Rock, The Rock." People just seemed to identify with him. He was immensely popular many years later.

What an impact he made when he came over from Cleveland! People just loved the guy. They loved his great throwing arm, and they loved his tape measure home runs—and Rocky rewarded the Tigers and their fans' faith in him with some of his best years.

Colavito was born in the Bronx and grew up a Yankees fan, in particular a huge fan of Joe DiMaggio. It was after DiMaggio that Rocky patterned his playing style, holding his bat high above his head like DiMaggio did and even copying Joltin' Joe's easy-gaited, loping, long-strided running style.

Rocky signed with Cleveland, and in 1956, his first full season, he captured the fancy of Indians fans when, as a 22-year-old, he belted 21 home runs and drove in 65 runs in 101 games. The following year, he hit 25 homers and drove in 84. In 1958, Colavito had 41 homers and 113 RBI. In '59, he tied with Harmon Killebrew for the American League lead in homers with 42, drove in 111, and on June 10 in Baltimore became the eighth player in baseball history and the third in the American League to hit four home runs in a game.

Then on April 17, 1960, came the unexpected and controversial trade that shocked Clevelanders. Colavito was sent to Detroit for Harvey Kuenn, the only time in baseball history a defending batting champion was traded for a defending home-run champion.

The people of Cleveland were outraged with the sudden, inexplicable departure of their favorite player and best hitter.

"What's all the fuss about?" asked Cleveland general manager Frank Lane, who had engineered the trade, and who, by then, had earned the nickname "Trader Lane." "All I did was trade hamburger for steak."

In response to Lane's comment, Tigers general manager Bill DeWitt, said, "I like hamburger."

As irate as Indians fans were with the deal, so too were some Tigers fans who preferred the consistency of the singles- and doubles-hitter Kuenn to the frequent strikeouts of the power-hungry Colavito. Although out-hit by Kuenn

Home-run king Rocky Colavito (second from left) was on the other end of the shocking trade that sent batting champion Harvey Kuenn to Cleveland. Here he and teammate Norm Cash talk shop with Yankees sluggers Roger Maris (left) and Mickey Mantle.

anywhere from 50 to 70 points, Colavito put up some big numbers in Detroit—35 homers and 87 RBI in 1960; career highs of a .290 average, 45 homers, and 140 RBI in 1961; and 37 homers and 112 RBI in 1962. But when he slipped to 22 homers and 91 RBI in 1963, Colavito was traded to Kansas City.

Colavito liked showing off his powerful throwing arm. Once, while playing for San Diego in the Pacific Coast League, he fired a ball from home plate clear over the center field wall, some 436 feet away. Twice during his career, he was called on to pitch in an emergency; the outings were 10 years apart, with the Indians in 1958 and the Yankees in 1968.

A right fielder in Cleveland, Colavito was forced to move to left field when he went to Detroit in deference to future Hall of Fame right fielder Al Kaline, but Rocky's throwing prowess continued, with 47 assists in four seasons.

When he retired, Colavito had 123 assists and 374 home runs, 371 in the American League, which placed him third on the AL's all-time list among right-handed hitters, behind Jimmie Foxx and Harmon Killebrew.

He also retired having pitched five and two-thirds innings in the major leagues, allowing one hit and with an earned-run average of 0.00 and a won-lost record of 1–0.

Leon Allen "Goose" Goslin didn't come to Detroit to be a star; he brought his star with him. In 13 seasons with the Washington Senators and St. Louis Browns, he had batted over .300 nine times, driven in more than 100 runs eight times, won a batting title and an RBI crown, and twice led the American League in triples.

In 1933, in his second tour in Washington, he helped the Senators win their first pennant in eight years by seven games over the Yankees.

Despite their success on the field, the Senators continued to struggle at the gate, and owner Clark Griffith ruefully admitted to Goslin that he couldn't afford to pay him what Goose was worth.

The Tigers had been floundering for almost a decade. Their fifth-place finish in '33 had been their sixth consecutive year in the second division of the American League. But there were indications that the Tigers' fortunes were on the upswing. Already in place were veterans Charlie Gehringer and Billy Rogell and pitchers Tommy Bridges, Schoolboy Rowe, and Elden Auker. And there was a new future star on the horizon in slugging first baseman Hank Greenberg. All the Tigers needed was a little tweaking.

Leon Goslin's (far left) arrival in 1934 provided the needed "goose" to elevate the Tigers from the doldrums of the American League to World Series contenders. Also pictured are (left to right) Charlie Gehringer, Hank Greenberg, and Pete Fox.

The first order of business was purchasing the contract of the great catcher Mickey Cochrane from the Philadelphia Athletics for $100,000 on December 12, 1933, making him the team's player/manager. Eight days later, the Tigers acquired Goslin from the strapped-for-cash Senators. By teaming Goslin with Gehringer and Greenberg in the middle of the batting order, the three Tigers came to be collectively known as "the G Men."

The change was miraculous. From a fifth-place team that won only 75 games, the Tigers were transformed into a powerhouse that won 101 games and captured their first pennant in 25 years by seven games over the Yankees. But the transformation was not complete, as the Tigers lost the World Series to the St. Louis Cardinals in seven games. There was still work to be done.

*I*f major league baseball were a once-a-week sport, played only on Sunday like professional football, Charlie Maxwell would be a Hall of Famer.
Instead, he is a former major leaguer with 14 years of service with the Red Sox, Orioles, White Sox, and Tigers, a two-time All-Star, an outstanding left fielder who twice led American League outfielders in fielding percentage, a Detroit fan favorite with an outgoing and engaging personality who liked to put on pregame shows for fans, especially kids, and, in his prime, one of the best power hitters in the American League.

Maxwell's career numbers are good: a .267 batting average, 148 home runs, 532 RBI.

But on Sundays, he was a superstar.

Forty of his 148 home runs, 27 percent, were hit on Sundays.

Maxwell was born in Lawton, a small town in western Michigan. Later, he made the city of Paw Paw, Michigan, his home and acquired "Paw Paw" as one of his nicknames. Others were "Smokey," "Sunday Charlie," and "the Sabbath Smasher."

After spending two years in the Army, Maxwell launched his professional baseball career when the Red Sox signed him as an amateur free agent in 1947. He would spend eight seasons in the Red Sox organization, mostly in the minor leagues. In Boston, he was used primarily as a backup to Ted Williams, not a situation ideally suited for regular employment or opportunity.

From 1950–54, Maxwell appeared in only 134 games for the Red Sox, and after the '54 season, he was sold to the Baltimore Orioles. He had played in only four games for Baltimore when, on May 9, 1955, he was sold to the Tigers.

Charlie Maxwell would find a haven with his hometown team. Over the next few years he would become one of the American League's most dangerous power hitters. A regular for the first time in his major league career, Maxwell batted .326 in 1956, hit 28 homers, drove in 87 runs, and had a slugging percentage of .534, third in the American League behind Mickey Mantle and Ted Williams.

He followed that up with 24 homers, 82 RBI, and a .276 average in 1957 but in 1958 fell off to .272 with 13 homers and 65 RBI, and Bill Norman, who had taken over as manager for the last two-thirds of the season, removed Maxwell as the Tigers' regular left fielder.

When the 1959 season began, Maxwell was tied to the bench, watching the Tigers get off to a horrendous start. They lost 15 of their first 17 games. Maxwell had started only four of the team's 17 games and pinch-hit in five others, but things were about to change.

On Sunday, May 3, Jimmie Dykes replaced Norman as manager with the Tigers scheduled to play a doubleheader at home against the New York Yankees.

"The problem," remembered Maxwell, who had gone 10 days without a start when Dykes arrived, "was that Norman didn't have the right team on the field. We had better guys on the bench than on the field. When Dykes took over, he asked the coaches, 'What's wrong with the Tigers?' And the coaches, Billy Hitchcock and Tommy Henrich, told him, 'We don't have our best team on the field.' So Dykes told the coaches, 'You make out the lineup,' which they did, and I got the start in left field, batting third in the first game of the doubleheader against the Yankees."

Maxwell singled in a run in the bottom of the third inning and hit a solo home run off Don Larsen in the seventh. In the second game, he hit a two-run home run off Duke Maas in the first inning, walked in the second, hit a three-run home run off Johnny Kucks in the fourth and a solo home run off Zack Monroe in the seventh for three home runs and six RBI in the game, home runs in four consecutive official at-bats, a single, a walk, and eight RBI in the doubleheader.

A legacy was born, and so, too, was a nickname: the Sabbath Smasher.

Maxwell would finish the season with a batting average of .251, 31 home runs (at the time, a Tigers record for home runs by a left-handed batter), and 95 RBI. Of his 31 home runs, Maxwell hit 12 on Sundays. He also batted .297 and drove in 34 runs on the Sabbath.

"I don't know why I hit so well on Sundays," Maxwell said. "I never could figure it out. The only thing I can think of is that all our Sunday games were played during the day. Back in that era, the lights were good but there always seemed to be a bit of a glow and I always felt I could pick the ball up better in day games."

In 1935, the Tigers won 93 games and their second straight pennant and took on the Chicago Cubs in the World Series. Leading the Series 3–2, the Tigers looked for the KO punch at home in Game 6. Batting in the bottom of the ninth with the score tied 3–3, manager Cochrane singled with one out and moved to second on Gehringer's grounder to first. That brought up Goslin, who had been hitless in four at-bats. He singled to right, and Cochrane came home to score the winning run that gave the Tigers their first world championship.

In two years, the G-Men combined for a staggering 114 home runs and 753 RBI.

Goslin would have one more good year for the Tigers, in 1936, with a .315 average, 24 homers, and 125 RBI before falling off to .238, four homers, and 35 RBI in 1937 and finishing out his career in Washington.

Goslin left the game with Hall of Fame numbers of a .316 batting average, 2,735 hits, 248 home runs, and 1,609 runs batted in. A New Jersey native, he also hit more home runs in the original Yankee Stadium, 32, than any other visiting player—a record that, with the completion of the new Yankee Stadium, will never be broken.

Put the name **Heinie Manush** on the list of terrible Tigers trades. In fairness, when the Tigers traded Manush after the 1927 season, it was because they had their usual outfield logjam and Manush was overshadowed by his more famous teammates Ty Cobb, Harry Heilmann, Bobby Veach, and Bob "Fatty" Fothergill.

Manush had burst onto the scene in Detroit as a 21-year-old rookie in 1923, forcing his way into part-time duty in that star-studded array by batting .334 and driving in 54 runs in 308 at-bats. Three years later, handpicked to replace the legendary but aging Ty Cobb as the team's center fielder by the Tigers' manager, Cobb himself, Manush became a full-fledged star. He came to the final day of the season in a four-way battle for the American League batting championship. With six hits in nine at-bats in a doubleheader, Manush surged into the lead and won the title with a .378 average, six points higher than Babe Ruth and 11 points ahead of his Tigers teammates, Heilmann and Fothergill.

When Manush "slumped" to .298 the following season—despite driving in 90 runs—he was traded to the St. Louis Browns, for whom he batted .378

Heinie Manush may have suffered comparisons to his better-known teammates such as Ty Cobb and Harry Heilmann, but he was a skilled player who would eventually receive a Hall of Fame induction.

and .355. Midway in the 1930 season, Manush was traded again, this time to the Washington Senators.

It was with Washington that Manush had his best years, batting .328 in more than 3,200 at bats. He finished his career with a lifetime average of .330, 110 home runs, and 1,183 RBI for 17 seasons and was elected to the Hall of Fame in 1964.

Statistical Summaries

All statistics are for player's Tigers career only.

HITTING

G = Games

H = Hits

HR = Home runs

RBI = Runs batted in

SB = Stolen bases

BA = Batting average

Left Fielder	Years	G	H	HR	RBI	SB	BA
Bobby Veach *Pitched two innings in final game of the 1918 season*	1912–23	1,604	1,859	59	1,042	189	.311
Willie Horton *Drove in a run in 10 consecutive games in 1976*	1963–77	1,515	1,490	262	886	14	.276
Rocky Colavito *Played in all 162 games without committing an error in 1965 for Cleveland*	1960–63	629	633	139	430	6	.271

continued	Years	G	H	HR	RBI	SB	BA
Goose Goslin *Hit into four double plays on 4/28/34*	1934–37	524	582	50	369	24	.297
Heinie Manush *His first major league homer came as pinch-hitter at Yankee Stadium on 6/20/23*	1923–27	615	674	38	345	48	.321

FIELDING

PO = Putouts

A = Assists

E = Errors

DP = Double plays

TC/G = Total chances divided by games played

FA = Fielding average

Left Fielder	PO	A	E	DP	TC/G	FA
Bobby Veach	3,431	190	134	39	2.4	.964
Willie Horton	1,905	58	55	8	1.7	.973
Rocky Colavito	1,278	47	23	10	2.2	.983
Goose Goslin	963	34	44	6	2.2	.958
Heinie Manush	1,179	33	37	7	2.4	.970

SEVEN

Center Fielder

Is **Ty Cobb** the greatest baseball player who ever lived? His admirers and supporters say he is.

Even many of his critics and detractors grudgingly point to his record to make the case that he is baseball's greatest player.

Cobb accomplished things no other player ever did, and when he left the game, he held 90 records—many of which still have not been equaled today, more than 80 years later...and likely never will be.

Cobb finished his 24-year career with the most games (3,035), at-bats (11,429), hits (4,191), runs (2,245), and stolen bases (892), all of which have been surpassed. But his lifetime batting average of .367, eight points better than Rogers Hornsby, remains the highest in baseball history, as does

1.	TY COBB
2.	CURTIS GRANDERSON
3.	CHET LEMON
4.	RON LEFLORE
5.	HOOT EVERS

his winning 11 batting championships (Honus Wagner and Tony Gwynn each won eight titles).

Cobb broke into the major leagues in 1905 and, at the age of 18, batted .240 in 41 games. But he never batted below .300 again in 23 seasons and twice batted over .400 (.420 in 1911 and .409 in 1912). In a 13-year period

Love him or hate him, Ty Cobb is inarguably one of the best to ever play the game. Here he slides spikes-up into an unidentified catcher.

from 1907–19, he won 11 batting titles and missed by an aggregate of 16 points of winning 13 straight. He finished second in 1910 to Napoleon Lajoie, .3840 to .3833, and second in 1916 to Tris Speaker, .386 to .371.

I've seen pictures of Cobb, and the one thing that jumps out at me is the way he batted with his hands held about two or three inches apart. It was not an uncommon practice back in Cobb's day, the so-called "dead-ball" era. Many hitters used that batting style as a means of gaining better bat control, which helps explain why batting averages were so high and home-run totals so low.

As great a hitter as he was, Cobb hit only 117 home runs in more than 11,000 at bats, and a good percentage of those were inside-the-park homers. His style of hitting was simply not conducive to home runs. Things began to change in the 1920s when Babe Ruth came along, grabbed headlines, and captured the attention and adulation of fans with his towering, out-of-the-park drives. Those Ruthian blasts were fan magnets because their like had never been seen before—which was precisely how Cobb viewed Ruth and his home runs, as fads with no staying power.

Proud and egotistical, Cobb became envious of Ruth's popularity. He condemned not only Babe's style of play but also his lifestyle, given as it was to excess. The more popular Ruth became, the more hostile toward him Cobb grew. Early in the 1925 season and at the age of 38, Cobb decided the time had come for him to prove a point. Smarting from the amount of attention the boisterous Ruth was garnering with his home runs, Cobb told a reporter that, for the first time, he was going to swing for the fences.

On May 5, in St. Louis, he had six hits in six at bats, including three home runs and five RBI. The next day, Cobb had three more hits in six at bats, two home runs, and six RBI. Within a four-game series against the Browns, Cobb had set a single-game American League record with 16 total bases, tied a major league record of five home runs in two games, and had nine consecutive hits. Once he had proved his point, he was ready to return to his preferred style of hitting.

Cobb was known as a fierce competitor, maybe the fiercest ever. He would do anything to win, within and outside the rules. Sportsmanship was never one of his traits. He used any device he could, the physical and psychological, to get the upper hand on an opponent. It's been said that before games he would sit in the Tigers' dugout in full view of opposing players and sharpen his spikes. Although this may or may not be true, it is true that he slid into bases hard and with spikes high.

So much about Cobb shows him to be a man of contradictions.

He was said to be a bigot, yet he praised Jackie Robinson's courage in breaking baseball's color line and told *The Sporting News,* "The Negro has a right to compete in sports, and who is to say they have not? They have been competing notably in football, track, and baseball, and I think they are to be complimented for their gentle conduct both on the field and, as far as I know, off the field." In addition, Cobb's substantial charitable contributions were largely responsible for the building of a hospital in his hometown and for a scholarship fund, both of which were open to African-Americans.

To many he is the most revered player in baseball history. To others he is the most reviled player in baseball history.

Tyrus Raymond (Ty) Cobb was many things to many people: combative, daring, surly, magnanimous, hostile, contradictory, enigmatic, compassionate, bigoted, self-absorbed, envious, belligerent, cunning, swashbuckling, intimidating, sagacious, profane, deceitful, ruthless, and crooked.

Above all, he was never dull, never ignored, and he was a towering figure in baseball's formative years.

Here, then, is a cross section of opinions about Ty Cobb, the man, the myth, and the baseball player: what others thought about him and what he thought about himself.

"C is for Cobb,
Who grew spikes and not corn,
And made all the basemen
Wish they weren't born."
                    —Ogden Nash

"Baseball is a red-blooded sport for red-blooded men. It's no pink tea, and mollycoddles had better stay out. It's a struggle for supremacy, survival of the fittest."

                                        —Ty Cobb

"Every time at bat for him was a crusade."

                                        —Charlie Gehringer

"Sure I fought. I had to fight all my life just to survive. They were all against me. Tried every dirty trick to cut me down, but I beat the bastards and left them in the ditch."

                                        —Ty Cobb

"The most sensational player of all the players I have seen in my life."

                                        —Casey Stengel

"Teach a boy to throw a baseball and he won't throw a rock."

—Ty Cobb

"He was the strangest of all of our national sports idols. But not even his disagreeable character could destroy the image of his greatness as a ballplayer. Ty Cobb was the best. That seemed to be all he wanted."

—Jimmy Cannon

"[Baseball is] not unlike war. If we can not only beat them but run wild on them in addition, treat them like a bunch of bush leaguers, it is liable to put them up in the air for a week."

—Ty Cobb

"Rarely should a baserunner risk a steal when the game is in balance. It's to be used when you can afford to fail."

—Ty Cobb

"I recall when Cobb played a series with each leg a mass of raw flesh. He had a temperature of 103, and the doctors ordered him to bed for several days, but he got three hits, stole three bases, and won the game."

—Grantland Rice

"Baseball was 100 percent of my life. I was a man who saw no point in losing if I could win. I never could stand losing. Second place didn't interest me. I had a fire in my belly. I loved the competition, the matching of muscle and wits. It was a joust and a challenge. Once an athlete feels the peculiar thrill that goes with victory and public praise, he's bewitched. He can never get away from it."

—Ty Cobb

"I often tried plays that looked recklessly daring, maybe even silly. But I never tried anything foolish when a game was at stake, only when we were far ahead or far behind. I did it to study how the other team reacted, filing away in my mind any observations for future use."

—Ty Cobb

"[Cobb] has brains in his feet."

—Branch Rickey

"[Hub Leonard, Boston Red Sox pitcher] would aim bullets at your head, left-handed, to boot...I dragged a bunt...which the first baseman was forced to field...Leonard sprinted for first to take the throw and saw that I was after him. He wouldn't have been safe that day if he'd scrambled into the top bleachers. I ignored the bag since I was already out, and dove feet first right through the coaching box. He managed to duck, but...the escape was close enough medicine for him. He never threw another beanball at me."

—Ty Cobb

"I may have been fierce, but never low or underhanded. The base paths belonged to me, the runner. The rules gave me the right. I always went into a bag full speed, feet first. I had sharp spikes on my shoes. If the baseman stood where he had no business to be and got hurt, it was his own fault."

—Ty Cobb

"The greatness of Ty Cobb was something that had to be seen, and to see him was to remember him forever."

—George Sisler

Although he amassed immense personal wealth with fortuitous, well-timed, and wise investments, including Coca-Cola and General Motors, Cobb was said to be notoriously frugal. Yet, without fanfare or publicity, he gave financial assistance to Tigers teammate Mickey Cochrane when the great catcher fell on hard times.

He was said to be antisocial and selfish, despised by opponents and teammates alike. He sustained a longtime feud with teammate Sam "Wahoo" Crawford. The two didn't speak for years, but it was later discovered that Cobb wrote many letters to baseball writers campaigning for Crawford's election to the Hall of Fame. Cobb also befriended a young Joe DiMaggio and counseled him during DiMaggio's contract dispute with the Yankees, even writing letters to Yankees general manager Ed Barrow on DiMaggio's behalf, stating his case for a pay increase.

Sadly, when Cobb died, only four men from baseball attended his funeral, a representative from the Hall of Fame and players Mickey Cochrane, Ray Schalk, and Nap Rucker.

After only a few years, **Curtis Granderson** showed so much talent and such a tremendous upside that I was willing to predict he would leapfrog over Doc Cramer, Hoot Evers, Billy Bruton, Ron LeFlore, Barney McCoskey, Mickey Stanley, Chet Lemon, and any other Tigers center fielder you can think of not named Ty Cobb. I still think he will do that, unfortunately he won't be doing it as a Tiger.

Circumstances and economics no doubt contributed to the Tigers having to trade Granderson to the New York Yankees, where I have no doubt he will continue blazing a trail to a stellar career. He has the potential to do so if he just keeps doing what he has been doing. He's a good outfielder who tracks the ball well and covers a lot of ground. I thought the same thing about Chet Lemon, but Curtis' offense gives him the edge over Chet.

In July 2005, the last season for Tigers manager Alan Trammell and his coaches, we had a couple of outfielders hurt and needed somebody to play center field, so Granderson was called up from Toledo in the International League. I didn't know much about him at the time. I had seen him in spring training and when he had come up for a few days the previous season, but he hadn't made much of an impression. This time it was different; he left a lasting impression in a very short time.

Granderson played in a four-game weekend series against the Twins and two games in Seattle, and he lit a fire under us with his speed, his enthusiasm, and his ability. We won four of six games with Curtis in the lineup—and this was a team that would end up losing 91 games. In the six games, he had seven hits, a .318 average, two triples, two home runs, scored four runs, drove in four runs, and played center field flawlessly. He did things I hadn't seen from our regular center fielder all season. Watching him I couldn't help thinking, *Why isn't this guy up here?*

The next thing we knew, our center fielder was healthy and Granderson was going to be sent back to Toledo. We were sitting around a conference table in the clubhouse talking about some moves we were going to make and I said, "I don't understand this. This guy is better than any center fielder we have. If we're trying to win games, why would we not keep him up here?"

Curtis Granderson has the potential to become a big star...but now he'll have to do it in a uniform other than the Tigers'.

The answer I got was that Granderson wasn't ready for the big leagues, before that year he had not played higher than Double A, he needed more seasoning…yada, yada, yada. So Curtis went back down to Toledo.

He came back again late that year and made a huge impression with an inside-the-park home run on September 15, a five-hit game on September 18, and a walk-off, game-winning home run on September 26. He played in 47 games, batted .272, hit eight home runs, and drove in 20 runs. Again, he was more productive than any other center fielder we had.

The Tigers finally made Granderson their regular center fielder in 2006, after Tram and his coaches were gone. It seemed like all the suggestions we made came to fruition the year after we were gone. Talk about timing being everything. We were on the outside looking in when Granderson batted a respectable .260, hit 31 doubles, nine triples, 19 home runs, drove in 68 runs as a lead-off man, and committed the first error of his major league career in his 151st game, the longest streak ever by a Tigers outfielder at the start of his career.

And he just keeps getting better. He garnered a .302 average in '07 with 38 doubles, a league-leading 23 triples (tied for the fourth most as a Tiger with Cobb and Sam Crawford), 23 homers, 74 RBI, and 26 stolen bases. He became the second player in major league history with at least 30 doubles, 20 triples, 20 homers, and 20 stolen bases in a season.

In '08, he batted .280, hit 26 doubles, again led the league in triples with 13, hit 22 homers, drove in 66, and stole 12 bases—all of that before his 28th birthday.

It was his breakout season. Curtis Granderson had become a star. The Tigers apparently thought so, too, because in the off-season they rewarded him with a five-year contract for more than $30 million.

The numbers Curtis has put up in his first three full seasons are no doubt impressive, but the numbers that catch my eye are Granderson's strikeouts, which he has reduced every year, from 174 in 2006 to 141 in '07 to 111 in '08. What that shows me is maturity, experience, baseball savvy, patience, and hard work, all of which will help Curtis keep getting better and better.

When the trade was made, Steve Kemp to the White Sox for **Chet Lemon**, soon after the end of the 1981 season, my reaction was, "You're trading *him*?" At the time, Kemp was one of our biggest stars. In five years with the Tigers, he had hit 89 home runs and driven in 422 runs. Twice he had knocked in more than 100 runs and hit more than 20 homers, big numbers in those days. When I first came up, it was always a big shock when they got rid of somebody who produced like that.

Obviously, the powers that be at the time—Jim Campbell, Bill Lajoie, and Sparky Anderson, who had just completed his second full year as manager in Detroit—were looking at the big picture: how to put a team together. They needed a center fielder, and Chet Lemon was a premier defensive player at the time who had been a pretty productive offensive player for the White Sox. He had set an American League record for outfielders in 1977 with 536 total chances and with 512 putouts (he would end his career with five seasons of at least 400 putouts, also an AL record).

The Tigers snatched him up in the prime of Chet's career, and he did a great job for us. He was a major contributor to our World Series championship team in 1984, his best year as a Tiger, with a .287 average, 20 home runs, and 76 RBI.

Lemon might be one of the best center fielders I've ever seen. He could track the ball down with the best of them. He had a strong arm, but it was a little erratic. I used to have more than my share of disagreements with him because he would never hit the cutoff man and would try to airmail the ball to the plate on a play at home.

When I was in the game and there was a play at the plate, I was into it. I wanted to get the guy out. And Chet, with his great arm, would throw the ball a mile from center field and he would often short-hop me, which drove me crazy. That's a do-or-die situation; you either get it or you don't. The times I didn't get it, I'd get angry because if he had just hit the cutoff man or at least even threw the ball a little farther out in front of me so I could play the hop, we would have had a better chance at getting the out at the plate.

I know in the heat of the game things like that often happen. I could understand it if it happened only in games, but Chet did the same thing during infield practice. In those days, we always had to take infield, not like today's game, when players take infield once in a blue moon. Under Sparky Anderson, if you didn't take infield, you couldn't play in the game. That was his rule. So we'd take infield practice every day, and every day Chet would short-hop me and I'd always get angry with him about it.

I can laugh about it now, but trust me, I wasn't laughing back then. Still, Chet was a great center fielder. In 1984, they said the Tigers were strong up the middle, and we were. Three of us, Alan Trammell, Lou Whitaker, and I, were already there. The fourth, Lemon, came later, and he was the missing piece of the puzzle. He was simply a great center fielder, and he had some productive years for us. He never matched the .318 season, 86 RBI, and the league-leading 44 doubles he had with the White Sox in 1979, but he was consistently in the .260 to .270 range, drove in between 60 and 80 runs, and his home-run production went up to 17 or more in six of his nine seasons in Detroit.

Chet Lemon covered the field better than most center fielders I've seen play the game.

Most important, he was a good clutch hitter who got some big hits for us. The one thing that surprised me about him is that for a guy who could run well and who played center field, he never stole a lot of bases—only 58 in 16 seasons and only once in double figures in a season.

One thing that drove Sparky crazy was that Chet would often dive head-first into first base on a ground ball to the infield. Some saw that as a sign of Chet's aggressiveness and hustle, but others, including Sparky, saw it as a dangerous and foolish maneuver. First, it doesn't get you to first base any faster. Second, and most important, it increases the risk of a shoulder injury or jammed, or even broken, fingers.

Lemon was also hit by pitches frequently—151 times in his career. In fact, in the decade of the 1980s, only Don Baylor was hit by a pitch more times than Lemon.

Chet left the game after the 1990 season, and soon after he retired he underwent some physical problems that resulted in the removal of his spleen. I'm pleased to say that Chet is doing well and is active in youth baseball in Eustis, Florida, his home. He coaches two AAU teams and is the head baseball coach for Eustis High School. Chet's son Marcus, a shortstop, played for his dad at Eustis High and was drafted in the fourth round by the Texas Rangers in the June 2006 draft.

The first time I saw **Ron LeFlore** was after I had first signed with the Tigers and was in extended spring training in Lakeland. One day some of the guys suggested we go over and watch the Lakeland Tigers play in a Florida State League game. The Tigers had signed LeFlore the year before, and he had played 32 games in Clinton, Iowa, and now was playing for Lakeland. He already had a reputation, so when he came up to bat, there was a buzz in the stands. I was paying attention.

I'll never forget it. He hit a ground ball to shortstop, and he was like a blur going to first base. I had never in my life seen a guy run that fast.

The Ron LeFlore story is well known. It was told in a book, *Breakout: From Prison to the Big Leagues,* which later became the basis for a CBS made-for-TV movie, *One in a Million: The Ron LeFlore Story,* starring LeVar Burton.

As told in the book, LeFlore grew up in a crime-riddled section of Detroit. His father was an alcoholic and absentee parent. His mother was a heroin addict but a hard-working woman and the sole financial support for her family. Ron's childhood was one of mingling with prostitutes, drug addicts and drug dealers, of drinking and committing petty robberies. He dropped out of school before reaching his teens, compiled a juvenile arrest record, and never took part in any sports. His first arrest came at age 15 on a minor charge. Later he was busted for armed robbery and sentenced to five to 15 years in Jackson State Penitentiary.

It was in prison that LeFlore, presumably to keep occupied, first played in an organized baseball league. Legend has it that Billy Martin, then managing the Tigers, was tipped off to LeFlore's skill and was coaxed into visiting the prison to scout LeFlore firsthand. Martin was so impressed with Ron's speed and strength that through his connections he arranged for LeFlore to receive a "day parole" to try out for the Tigers in the summer of 1973.

Once again, LeFlore put on a show, this time for Tigers brass, who offered Ron a contract. That met the conditions for Ron's parole, which required that LeFlore have gainful employment, and it enabled him to get his release from prison that July. The Tigers sent LeFlore to Clinton, Iowa, to finish out

Ron LeFlore had little experience playing baseball, but his sheer speed alone grabbed the attention of major league scouts. *Courtesy of AP Images*

the Midwest League schedule. In 32 games, he batted .277 and the following year was promoted to Lakeland in the Florida State League, where I first saw him.

Ron was ahead of me in the Tigers' farm system, so it was a while before I saw him again. One fall I was sent to the Instructional League in Florida, and LeFlore was there. I remember being in the clubhouse, where we were changing from our street clothes to our uniforms. I happened to look over at LeFlore and saw him stripped to the waist. What a sight! He had a physique like Charles Atlas times two. It reminded me of looking at a racehorse and seeing all the veins popping out in the horse's legs. LeFlore had veins popping out of every part of his body. He could have been one of those bodybuilders. He didn't even look human. He was so big and muscular that I couldn't get over it.

As I got to know him and as he became more comfortable around the other players, Ron told us stories about his time in Jackson. The guards would take the inmates on work details where they had to pick potatoes. One day they came to get LeFlore for the detail and he said, "I ain't doing it. I'm not picking potatoes any more." He told us that they beat the crap out of him and threw him in solitary confinement, leaving him there until he changed his mind.

He said that he couldn't sleep in prison because guys would scream all night long and keep everybody awake. It was driving him out of his mind, so he decided to do something throughout the day to make himself so physically exhausted that he'd be able to pass out at night and sleep.

He did push-ups and sit-ups all day long until he was absolutely spent. He said he did fingertip push-ups—where he had his arms extended in front of him and he lifted his body on his fingertips. He even demonstrated those push-ups in case we didn't believe him. But I'll tell you what, looking at his phenomenal physique, I wouldn't doubt anything he said about how he got that way.

People have asked me if it was intimidating to be a teammate of someone who served time for armed robbery. My answer is that it might have been if it had been anybody but Ron LeFlore. He had a way of lightening the atmosphere. He always had a smile on his face, he was always joking around, and even though you knew his history, when you were around him, he was just a regular guy and you couldn't help but like him. I couldn't even imagine him doing the things for which he was imprisoned. If anything intimidated you, it was his physical presence. He was just a guy out for a good time who was enjoying freedom wherever he was.

One moment he was in solitary confinement and the next he was a major league baseball player. It's a totally different world, like going from the proverbial outhouse to the penthouse. No wonder he was smiling all the time.

Ron was not a natural athlete. Except for his speed, he had to work to be a good baseball player. He's the best I've ever seen at beating the throw to second base after getting picked off first. So many times I saw him get picked off first, then the pitcher would throw to the first baseman and, more often than not, Ron would beat the first baseman's throw to be safe at second.

Ron had a pretty good career, all things considered. With the Tigers, he had four very productive years from 1976 to 1979, batting .316, .325, .297, and .300. He made the All-Star team in '76, led the American League in runs scored and stolen bases, and set a still-standing Tigers record of 27 consecutive successful stolen bases in '78. Because of his speed, he was a perfect leadoff man, but he also had a high on-base percentage (over .355 for each of those four seasons) and he was strong enough to hit the ball out of the ballpark.

In those four seasons, he had 762 hits, 205 walks, 243 stolen bases, 41 home runs, and 215 RBI. After the 1979 season, Ron was traded to Montreal, where he spent one season. He then spent the last two years of his career with the White Sox. All told, his major league career was nine years—and a great deal better than what the alternative for him might have been.

By all accounts, **Hoot Evers** should have had a much better career than he did, but a series of bad breaks, misfortune, and poor timing hampered him. Evers was a star player at the University of Illinois at Urbana-Champaign and a much sought-after prospect when the Tigers signed him in 1941. He got into one game with the Tigers as a September call-up and then spent the next four years in military service during World War II.

Losing those four years at a young age when he might have been learning his trade in the minor leagues and on the big-league level impeded his progress. Nevertheless, when he returned from service in 1946, Hoot (he got

Injuries and circumstances kept Hoot Evers from what would have otherwise been an outstanding career.

the name as a child because he loved watching movies of cowboy star Hoot Gibson) took over as the Tigers' starting center fielder. He was doing well—batting in the .260s, showing some power, playing good defense—but midway through the season he broke his ankle and was out for the remainder of the year.

Evers came back to bat .296 with 10 homers and 67 RBI in 1947 and then hit over .300 in each of the next three seasons. In 1948, he batted .314 with 10 homers and 103 RBI and was the starting center fielder in the All-Star Game. In his first at-bat, he hit a home run off Ralph Branca.

Evers had his best season in 1950, with a .323 average, 21 home runs, and 103 RBI. He led the American League in triples and AL outfielders in fielding percentage, .997, with one error in 341 chances.

For some unknown reason, Evers' bat went cold the following year. His average dropped off 99 points to .224, his home runs dipped from 21 to 11, and his RBI from 103 to 46. In midseason of the following year, he was part of a blockbuster nine-man trade between the Tigers and the Red Sox.

Hoot would come back to the Tigers in 1954, purchased from the Giants off the waiver wire. He would finish out his career with the Orioles and Indians. When his playing career ended, he stayed with Cleveland as a coach and in their front office until he returned to Detroit as director of player development in 1971. In that capacity, he was a familiar figure around Detroit, in the minor leagues, and in spring training and was instrumental in bringing to the Tigers, under his watch, Alan Trammell, Lou Whitaker, Ron LeFlore…and a young catcher named Parrish.

When I knew him, Hoot was a cranky old guy, but I loved him. I felt bad for him because at that time, he suffered the worst migraine headaches, and that probably made him more irritable than he already was.

I enjoyed being around Hoot, even though I wasn't around him for more than five minutes when he chewed my butt out for the first time. I had just signed my contract and was to report to Lakeland for extended spring training before starting my professional career in rookie ball. A week after I graduated from high school, I was on a red-eye from Los Angeles to Tampa.

There I was, just a couple of days past my 18th birthday, away from home alone for the first time in my life and in Florida for the first time. When I got off the plane, I felt like I was on another planet. It was so humid I couldn't believe it. I had been told that when I arrived in Tampa, I was to find the airport shuttle and tell the driver I needed to go to Tigertown in Lakeland, so that's what I did.

It took about two hours to get there. When I got to Tigertown, my first stop was to check in at Fetzer Hall, the complex that included dormitory rooms, a cafeteria, and a lounge. I hadn't had any sleep. I was fried. I was tired. I was hungry. I was hot from the humidity. And I was distraught because I was away from my family, on my own for the first time in my life. All I wanted to do was lay down in an air-conditioned room and sleep, but when I checked in, the guy at the desk said, "Here's your room key. You can put your bags in the room. They're serving breakfast right now in the cafeteria."

I went to the cafeteria and got something quick to eat, shoveled it down, and then headed back to my room. I was thinking, *I've got to go to bed.* I was ready to pass out. I jumped into bed—I just wanted to take a nap—and the next thing I knew—Bam! There came somebody busting through my door.

I didn't even know who the guy was—and he's screaming at me in this gruff voice, "What the hell are you doing in bed? We've got a workout over at the stadium. You can sleep when you're done. We're having a workout and it started 10 minutes ago, so you better get your butt over there."

That was my introduction to Hoot Evers. I think deep down he liked me and he championed me. Early in my career in the minor leagues, I didn't have the greatest success, but Hoot stuck with me and pushed me. I got to see a different side of him later on, and I came to really like him.

When I first saw him, I didn't know who he was or what he did. I came to find out that he had been a pretty good player, and that gave a lot of credibility to the things he told me along the way. And the more I got to know him, the more I liked him.

Statistical Summaries

All statistics are for player's Tigers career only.

HITTING

G = Games

H = Hits

HR = Home runs

RBI = Runs batted in

SB = Stolen bases

BA = Batting average

Center Fielder	Years	G	H	HR	RBI	SB	BA
Ty Cobb *Had five or more hits in a game a record 14 times*	1905–26	2,806	3,900	111	1,804	865	.368
Curtis Granderson *Tripled and scored the game-winning run in 2009 All-Star Game*	2004–09	674	702	102	299	67	.272
Chet Lemon *Led league in hit by pitch three straight years (1981–83)*	1982–90	1,203	1,071	142	536	13	.265

continued	Years	G	H	HR	RBI	SB	BA
Ron LeFlore *Had a 30-game hitting streak in 1976 and a 27-game streak two years later*	1974–79	787	970	51	265	294	.297
Hoot Evers *Only hit for 1954 World Champion Giants was a three-run walkoff HR on June 19*	1941, 46 52, 54	769	787	63	429	35	.290

114

FIELDING

PO = Putouts

A = Assists

E = Errors

DP = Double plays

TC/G = Total chances divided by games played

FA = Fielding average

Center Fielder	PO	A	E	DP	TC/G	FA
Ty Cobb	5,964	376	257	105	2.4	.957
Curtis Granderson	1,724	25	13	7	2.6	.993
Chet Lemon	2,637	53	34	14	2.6	.988
Ron LeFlore	1,947	62	56	14	2.8	.973
Hoot Evers	1,853	57	33	8	2.7	.983

EIGHT

Right Fielder

Nobody is more closely identified with Detroit Tigers baseball than Mr. Tiger himself, **Al Kaline**, who has spent more than half a century with the Tigers as a player, television analyst, and special assistant to the president. One cannot be in Detroit for much time before discovering that Al Kaline is as much a part of the Detroit Tigers organization as any individual.

My first year in the Detroit organization, 1974, was Kaline's last as a player. But even after he retired, he was a familiar face at spring training and was consistently involved in just about everything the Tigers did. That's why he's Mr. Tiger.

His contributions to Tigers lore transcends those from his playing career—which is not to minimize what he did as a player. He had a fabulous 22-year career, all of them with the Tigers,

1.	AL KALINE
2.	HARRY HEILMANN
3.	SAM CRAWFORD
4.	KIRK GIBSON
5.	MAGGLIO ORDOÑEZ

and is a worthy recipient of Hall of Fame induction—unless you think a .297 lifetime batting average, 3,007 hits, 399 home runs, 1,583 runs batted in, three years with at least 100 RBI, 20 straight years of home runs in double figures, nine seasons with a batting average of .300 or better, 15 All-Star selections, and

10 Gold Gloves (tied with Ken Griffey Jr., for the most by an American League outfielder) are easy to come by.

As a Tiger, Kaline has played the most games, hit the most home runs, drawn the most walks, and hit the most sacrifice flies. He is second to Ty Cobb in at-bats, hits, total bases, extra-base hits, and RBI.

Al was one of the early "bonus babies," back before there was a draft and every player was a free agent. The Tigers scouted Kaline as a high school player in Baltimore and signed him as soon as he was eligible—on the night of his high school graduation, June 19, 1953—for a bonus of $35,000. Six days later, at 18 years, six months, and six days, he was in Philadelphia with the Tigers and in their starting lineup as right fielder against the Athletics.

Among his Tiger teammates were Bob Swift, who was 38; Billy Hitchcock, 36; Ray Scarborough 35; and Johnny Pesky, Pat Mullin, Hal Newhouser, and Jerry Priddy, all in their 30s. Some of them might have had kids who were nearly Kaline's age.

I wonder how those veteran players responded to him. I can imagine them thinking, *I have kids in high school and this guy's just out of it and he's my teammate?!*

Kaline has a long list of accomplishments, including being elected to the Hall of Fame, but let's face it, you may run into Hall of Fame players from time to time—there are enough of them around—but how many guys went straight from high school to the big leagues? That's a huge step, and it says a lot about his ability and his maturity.

I can't even imagine going straight from high school to the major leagues without ever playing a game in the minors. Looking back, I know that there is absolutely no way I could have done it. I'm awed by anyone who does—and especially to play at such a high level as Kaline. It boggles my mind.

Like Kaline, I also signed when I was 18, but my first stop was in a rookie league, not the major leagues. I thought I was "it" when I made it to the Tigers at the age of 21; at that age Kaline was already in his fourth major league season, had made the All-Star team twice, and had won a batting title. In 1955, he hit .340 with 200 hits, and at the age of 20 he became the youngest player in major league history to win a batting championship, just 12 days younger than another Tiger great, Ty Cobb, who won the title in 1907.

After he retired from playing, I remember him at spring training as a special instructor working with the hitters. As great a player as he was and as much as he could offer us hitters, I still felt that he was there to stay a part of the game.

Al Kaline is and always will be Mr. Tiger.

Observations from Mr. Tiger, himself, Al Kaline:

I'll never forget that first night with the team. Going to the ballpark on the bus was the hardest 30 minutes of my life. I had to walk down that aisle between all the players. I really didn't know too much about the Tigers at the time. I didn't know who was on the team, but I saw every eye as I walked down the aisle. It looked like a thousand eyes were staring right at me and saying, "Who is this young punk?" I just kept my eyes straight ahead.

All of a sudden I'm in the major leagues and we're traveling from town to town. I see the other players dressing different every day. I've got only one suit, and I keep wearing it over and over. I'm really embarrassed.

As the days went on, I didn't mind the games. In fact, I looked forward to them. That was the easiest part of all. I couldn't wait to get to the ballpark. I'd be the first one there, and I was willing to do anything. I think that's why the veterans liked me.

I started in for the ball, but I just couldn't get it. I should have caught it because I used to catch everything on the sandlots. But they hit the ball a lot harder in the major leagues, and I just couldn't reach the ball this time.

Baseball is a great job. You play six months a year and people do everything for you. All you have to do is play the games.

I was at a young age and the writers...started comparing me to Cobb. It put a lot of pressure on me.

I'd always heard what a fierce man Ty Cobb was, but when I met him he was very mild-mannered. He told me, "Always bear down because there'll come a time when you won't be able to bear down," meaning that there'll come a time when you won't be able to play.

If you think you can hit, two strikes won't mean anything to you.

The secret of being a good hitter is to wait for your pitch to hit and then hit it.

I don't deserve such a salary [in 1971, the Tigers offered to make Kaline the first $100,000 player in franchise history]. I didn't have a good season last year. This ballclub has been so fair and decent to me that I'd prefer to have you give it to me when I rate it [Kaline earned a $100,000 salary in 1972].

I was very, very shocked about Cooperstown. I thought my chances were fairly good, but I tried to stay low key about it, not too high and not too low. That was the way I played, too.

What gets me upset about the newer players is their lack of intensity. They tend to go through the motions a little bit. They don't understand that you've got to practice the way you play. You've got to get good habits of working hard so that when that play comes up, you're able to complete it and do it the right way.

Observations about Mr. Tiger, Al Kaline:

"There's a hitter. In my book, he's the greatest right-handed hitter in the league."

—Ted Williams, 1955

"The kid murders you with his speed and arm. He's made some catches I still don't believe. I sort of hate to think what'll happen when he grows up."
—Casey Stengel, 1955

"No he did not. He was a gentleman. It would have to be a real borderline pitch for him to even turn his head."
—Umpire Larry McCoy, when asked if Kaline ever argued one of his calls

"I wouldn't trade him for Mantle or Mays."
—Bob Scheffing, Tigers manager, 1961–63

"I don't want to sound like one of those guys who manages in Chicago and says this Chicago player is the best, then manages in St. Louis and says this St. Louis player is the best. But I've been watching Kaline…and he's the best player who ever played for me. Jackie Robinson was the most exciting runner I ever had…and Hank Aaron was the best hitter. But for all-around ability, I mean hitting, fielding, running, and throwing, I'll go with Al."
—Charlie Dressen, Tigers manager, 1963–66

He seemed to be hesitant to get involved in instruction. I think he did it only because the Tigers asked him to. I got the impression that he didn't want to insinuate himself on people or usurp the authority and duties of the coaches. He was respectful of them and the job they had to do, and he was careful not to step on anyone's toes or override anyone's authority. He was still that way when I became a coach. If asked specifically by one of the coaches to do something, he would gladly oblige, but he would never jump in and say, "You have to do it this way." He seemed hesitant to cross that boundary, though I doubt anyone would have been offended. After all, he *is* Al Kaline.

I can remember times when I was struggling as a hitter. If I saw Al on the field, I wouldn't hesitate to ask for his help. But he would never offer suggestions unless he was asked. To me, that was an indication of his humility and his genuine concern and consideration for others.

Kaline never got wrapped up in his own celebrity. Obviously, he's a superstar, but I think he tries to distance himself from that attention. Even though he's always cordial when people ask him for an autograph, he won't make a show of it like some guys and stand there and sign 100 autographs. He might in passing stop and sign a few and go on his way, but he maintains a private side.

People might misread that, but I have come to know him as a kind person— I have never heard him say a bad word about anybody—who is a very astute and knowledgeable baseball guy (and believe me, not every superstar is). When I was a coach for the Tigers, Al would sit in on our meetings and make some very sagacious observations; everybody respected his opinions.

I've always held the impression that he was more comfortable out of the limelight. I'm sure he appreciates that people still hold him in high regard, but I believe he'd just as soon stay back in the shadows. However, being Al Kaline, that would be difficult for him to do—especially in Detroit. Kaline has always made himself available to promote the Detroit Tigers for just about anything and everything they do, from attending fantasy camps to going on press tours. He's been a huge help to the Tigers' organization.

I can truthfully say that during my playing days, he was extremely helpful to me in my career, and I know he was helpful to others. I have the greatest respect for him, and he has my gratitude. There's just one thing. He has, through the years, consistently kicked my butt on the golf course. And he loves doing it and then rubbing it in. He's a heckuva golfer, good enough to play in Pro-Am tournaments. I'm a guy who gets out there and tries to hit it as far as I can; Al is a finesse player who scores better than everyone he plays with. He strives to be as much of a perfectionist on the golf course as he was on the baseball field. As far as I'm concerned, he's unbeatable.

I never saw him play baseball, but I learned a lot about him from talking to many who did. People talk about what a great hitter he was, what a great outfielder he was. They say Al Kaline never made a bad throw or missed a cutoff man; he was always pinpoint accurate throwing from the outfield.

When Kirk Gibson came along, Kaline came to spring training and worked with Gibby on his routes, how to make his turns when he was reading balls, which way to turn to throw and hit the cutoff man after fielding a ball…all the aspects of outfield play. Kirk responded well to Kaline's instruction and became a better outfielder because of it.

In short, when it comes to the Detroit Tigers, the first name on everybody's lips is Al Kaline. He was the first Tiger to have his number (No. 6) retired. A street behind Tiger Stadium is named for him. He is easily the most popular player to ever play for the Tigers and probably the most popular Detroit athlete ever. Everybody still loves him.

At another time, in another place, **Harry Heilmann** might be regarded as one of the four or five greatest hitters in baseball history. As it is, he gets high marks as a hitter, along with Ed Delahanty, Napoleon Lajoie, Honus Wagner, Al Simmons, and Rogers Hornsby, considered the greatest right-handed hitters in the game's formative years.

But like "Wahoo" Sam Crawford, Bobby Veach, and Heinie Manush, Heilmann was overshadowed and overwhelmed as a teammate of the irrepressible Ty Cobb.

Heilmann and Cobb played together for 12 seasons, and Cobb outhit his younger teammate in each of their first six years together. In the next six years, Heilmann had the edge on his aging teammate five times.

It wasn't until 1921, his seventh big-league season, that Heilmann finally overtook Cobb and won his first of four batting titles with a .394 average, five points higher than Cobb, the runner-up. Heilmann's three other batting titles would come in alternating years, 1923, '25, and '27.

Harry Heilmann was one of the biggest bats on the hitter-rich Detroit teams of the 1910s and 1920s.

In 1923 he beat out Babe Ruth by 10 points to win his second hitting crown with a .403 average, becoming the sixth player in the modern era and the first right-handed batter to hit over .400.

A third batting title came two years later with a .393 average that was four points higher than Tris Speaker. Cobb, at .378, finished fourth.

In 1927, after Cobb had moved on to the Philadelphia Athletics, Heilmann won the last of his four batting titles with a .398 average, six points better than Simmons.

Heilmann was one of the few teammates—or opponents, for that matter—who had a close relationship with the irascible, cantankerous, and egomaniacal Cobb. It should be pointed out that Heilmann won his first three batting titles when Cobb was the Tigers' player/manager, so Cobb had a vested interest in Heilmann's success. In later years Heilmann often credited Cobb with his own improvement in hitting.

Heilmann came out of San Francisco, a fertile area for baseball players (the DiMaggios, Lefty O'Doul, Joe Cronin, Tony Lazzeri, and Ping Bodie, to name a few). At 19, he was working as a bookkeeper for a biscuit maker when a former high-school teammate asked Heilmann to fill in for a player on a team in the San Joaquin Valley League. A scout for the Portland Beavers of the Northwest League saw him hit an eleven inning game-winning double and offered Heilmann a contract. When he batted .305 for Portland in 1913, his contract was sold to the Tigers for $1,500.

In the beginning, Heilmann shuttled between Detroit and San Francisco of the Pacific Coast League until returning to the Tigers to stay (and launch his sensational career) in 1916. In Detroit, he batted over .300 for 11 straight seasons, drove in more than 100 runs eight times, and won those four batting titles. After the 1929 season he was sold to Cincinnati, where he spent two years and finished out his career.

Heilmann retired with a lifetime batting average of .342, (12th on the all-time list and second in the modern era to Hornsby, among right-handed hitters), 183 home runs, and 1,539 RBI. On the Tigers' all-time list, he is second in batting average and slugging percentage, third in RBI, and fourth in on-base percentage, hits, total bases, doubles, triples, and extra-base hits.

A whole new generation of fans came to know, and revere, Heilmann when he joined the Tigers' broadcast team in 1934. He remained on Tigers radio broadcasts for 17 years, earning enormous popularity throughout the state of Michigan because of his humor, his knowledge of the game, and his ability to weave amusing and interesting stories into his play-by-play broadcasts.

In the spring of 1950, Heilmann was diagnosed with throat cancer but managed to return to the broadcast booth sporadically during the season. That summer, Cobb launched a letter-writing campaign to members of the Baseball Writers Association, appealing to them to elect Heilmann to the Hall of Fame while he was still alive (Cobb had conducted a similar campaign on behalf of Sam Crawford, a teammate to whom he had not spoken for years).

With the help of Cobb's pleas to the writers, Heilmann's vote total jumped from 87 (51.8 percent) in 1950 to 153 (67.7 percent) in 1951 but still left him 17 votes short of election.

The 1951 All-Star Game was scheduled to be played in Detroit on July 10. A day before the game, Heilmann, who had planned to attend, passed away.

Six months later, in January 1952, Heilmann was elected to the Hall of Fame posthumously with 203 votes and 86.8 percent of the ballots.

The first major star of the Detroit Tigers, even before Ty Cobb, was **"Wahoo" Sam Crawford**, who joined the team in 1903, two years before Cobb arrived, as part of a peace settlement between the established National League and the upstart American League.

Crawford had been a star in the National League with the Cincinnati Reds from 1899 until 1902 and hit an unheard-of 16 home runs in 1901. After the 1902 season, a bidding war broke out between the two leagues, and Crawford jumped to Detroit, setting off a legal dispute. Eventually, the two leagues buried the hatchet, and as part of the peace agreement, Crawford was allowed to remain with the Tigers. He would stay with them for 15 years and become one of the new league's biggest stars.

Crawford finished second in the league in batting in 1903, '07, and '08 when he led the American League in home runs with seven, making him the first player to win home-run crowns in each league.

Cobb arrived in 1905 and teamed with Crawford to give the Tigers the most fearsome one-two punch in the American League, Cobb batting third and Crawford fourth. Together, they were instrumental in leading the Tigers to three consecutive pennants, from 1907 to '09.

Having Cobb bat ahead of him helped Crawford to lead the AL in RBI three times, in 1910, '14, and '15.

Although they were teammates for parts of 13 seasons, played side-by-side in the outfield, hit back-to-back in the batting order, and worked in concert on several base-running plays, Crawford and Cobb had an uneasy and strained relationship, though it hadn't started out that way. When Cobb joined the Tigers, he looked up to Crawford as an established star and sought his advice, which Crawford willingly gave. Years later, Cobb told his biographer how much he appreciated the advice and kindness of Crawford.

As Cobb grew in stature, his relationship with Crawford changed. They became jealous rivals. Crawford reportedly resented the preferential treatment Cobb received—being allowed to report late for spring training, and given private and luxurious room accommodations on the road.

Sam Crawford's career 312 triples is still a major league record nearly 100 years later.

Crawford charged that if he had two or three hits in a game and Cobb went hitless, Cobb would fume and sometimes leave the ballpark before the game was over. Cobb retaliated with charges that Crawford often intentionally fouled off pitches when Cobb was stealing a base.

After the 1917 season, the Tigers released Crawford. He left with a lifetime average of .309 and still-standing major league records of 312 career triples, 12 inside-the-park home runs in a season, and 51 in his career. His major league days were behind him, but Crawford was not quite ready to stop playing. He signed with the Los Angeles Angels and helped them win Pacific Coast League championships in 1918 and 1921. In 1919, he batted .360 for the Angels with 239 hits, 41 doubles, 18 triples, 14 home runs, and 14 stolen bases. In 1920, he again had 239 hits, as well as 46 doubles and 21 triples. And in 1921, at the age of 41, he had 199 hits and 44 doubles.

Crawford remained in California and became head baseball coach at the University of Southern California from 1924–29. From 1935–38, he was an umpire in the Pacific Coast League.

When he retired as an umpire, Crawford lived as a recluse. In 1957, reporters tracked him to a cabin on the edge of the Mojave Desert to inform him that he had been elected to the Baseball Hall of Fame. When contacted by Hall of Fame officials, Crawford had one request. "I want my plaque to read, 'Wahoo Sam,'" he said. "That's my hometown [Wahoo, Nebraska] and I'm proud of it."

I have probably played with a couple of thousand guys in sandlot ball, Little League, high school, the minor leagues, and the majors, but there is nobody I ever played with who hated losing more than **Kirk Gibson**.

Guys can say they hate to lose—I have heard it hundreds of times—but just to watch Gibby in action, you realized that wasn't just lip service. He could come in the clubhouse after having a great day at the plate and on the field, but if we lost the game, you would be well advised to approach him with caution because he might just go off because we lost.

Kirk is easily the most intense baseball player I've ever been around. That intensity obviously comes from his experience as a football player—and he was a good one at Michigan State—where you played only one game a week and 11 games a season, and every one was crucial.

Even though he played only one season of college baseball, Gibby was drafted in the first round, 12th overall, in the June 1978 baseball free-agent draft by the Tigers and in the seventh round of the NFL draft by the St. Louis Cardinals as a wide receiver. He could have been drafted higher in both sports, but some baseball teams backed off because he still had a year of football eligibility remaining, and some football teams backed off because he was such a high draft pick in baseball.

In his senior year at Michigan State, Gibson led the Spartans football team to a tie for the Big Ten title while setting Michigan State and Big Ten

Kirk Gibson is one of the fiercest competitors I have ever played with or against.

receiving records, starring in the Hula Bowl and Senior Bowl, and making the most important All-America teams. Gil Brandt of the Dallas Cowboys said he believed Kirk should have won the Heisman Trophy, but because Michigan State was on probation and the Spartans were banned from having their games on national television, Gibson did not get the TV exposure that would have been witnessed by voters across the country.

Gibson eventually opted for baseball over football, influenced no doubt by the Tigers' bonus of $120,000 and the knowledge that a baseball player's career is generally longer than a football player's. But Gibby never lost that football mentality; he brought it with him into baseball. He could be downright surly. I used to feel sorry for the reporters who were sent into the clubhouse to talk to him. He wasn't the nicest interview. He always told them what he thought, particularly if he was in a bad mood over a loss. I remember a lot of occasions when Kirk got in reporters' faces. There was never a question where he was coming from.

If he had a bad day and the team won, he was okay. He was always intense and on edge, but when we won he was in a better mood. He just loved to win.

When Gibson came to the Tigers in 1979, he was a raw but obviously gifted athlete who ran faster and hit a ball farther than anybody I had ever seen. I remember him working out in Detroit before he signed, and the word was out that the Tigers were thinking of drafting this big football star from Michigan State. So, out of curiosity, some of us went out to check him out. What a show he put on! He must have hit 50 balls into the upper deck. He was just pummeling them. I'm not overstating this. Kirk would put balls into orbit. I remember him hitting a ball against Tom Seaver in old Comiskey Park in Chicago that went through the light tower in right-center field. It was one of those shots where you just say, "Holy cow!" It just disappeared into the night.

Run? The NFL combine got him at 4.2 for the 40-yard dash. That's world-class speed. He's the only guy I've ever seen tag up from second base on a fly ball and score, and he did that a few times that I can remember. You take anybody—Ron LeFlore, Bo Jackson, Willie Wilson, Willie Davis, Mickey Mantle, anybody—and I'd put my money on Gibson, whether they were running 90 feet or five miles. For me to be convinced that anyone could outrun him, I'd have to see it with my own eyes. He was that fast.

And he was competitive! In spring training, we would run laps around the field, Sparky Anderson's idea of getting us in shape for the season. We'd start out running a couple of laps, and as spring training progressed, it went from a couple of laps to three or four laps to five or six laps.

To make it interesting, guys who were in shape, mainly pitchers, would try to beat Gibson, but they never could. Kirk always, *always*, had to be first. He hated to lose in anything, and he never let anybody beat him running those laps. Guys would stay with him until the last few yards and then try to out-sprint him to the finish, but he would take off and leave them in the dust every time. It was phenomenal, and it was a fun thing to watch.

Kirk played only 143 games in the minor leagues when he came up to the Tigers to stay at the end of the 1979 season. Two years later, in 83 games, he batted .328, and people started calling him "another Mickey Mantle."

Though he had a productive career, you'd have to say that overall he never reached the level of success that his talent indicated he would reach. I'm surprised he never put up monster numbers because I believe he was that good. Except for the .328 in 83 games in 1981, he never hit .300, he never drove in 100 runs, and he never hit more than 29 home runs. In other words, he never came close to matching Mickey Mantle except for one thing: like Mantle, he lost a lot of time because of injuries. In Kirk's first tenure with the Tigers, from 1980 (his first full season) to 1987 (he came back and was a part-time player with them in '93–'95), he played in only 881 games out of a possible 1,242, mostly because of injuries. Effectively, he missed about one out of every three games.

One thing you have to say about Gibby, however, is that he certainly had a flair for the dramatic.

All baseball fans have seen film clips of his home run off Dennis Eckersley in Game 1 of the 1988 World Series. It's one of the most dramatic home runs in baseball history.

Kirk was with the Dodgers at the time. He had a terrific season that year, but a leg injury kept him out of the starting lineup for Game 1 of the World Series. He could hardly walk, let alone run. The Dodgers went into the bottom of the ninth inning trailing 4–3, and Oakland brought in Dennis Eckersley, who was practically a sure thing as a closer that year. In the regular season he saved 45 games, and in the American League Championship Series, he saved all four games in a four-game sweep of the Red Sox, allowing no runs and only one hit. He was the closest thing to unhittable.

Eck got the first two batters easily, and then he walked pinch-hitter Mike Davis. That put the tying run on first base, the winning run at the plate. With the pitcher due up, Dodgers manager Tommy Lasorda sent Kirk up to pinch-hit, knowing that with his bad leg, if Gibby hit the ball on the ground, there was no way he could run to first base. He might not even have been able to get to first if he hit a line-drive single to the outfield. Lasorda was gambling on one thing: the long ball.

My wife and I were at home, watching the game on television, and we saw Gibby limping out of the dugout. Having played with him as many years as I did and having seen him come up with some big hits and big home runs when he was a Tiger, and knowing his abilities, it didn't matter to me that he was going to bat on one leg. I had seen how strong he was, probably one of the strongest guys I've ever seen in the game as far as hitting a baseball a great distance. I knew that if he could just get his bat on the ball, he had a chance to hit it out of the ballpark.

But I didn't think that was going to happen. I remember saying to my wife, "If he hits the ball out of the park, I'll die." Just like that. And then a few pitches later, with the count 3–2, Bam! You've got to be kidding. You couldn't have scripted it any better.

I was happy for Kirk. It was a great moment, one of the greatest in World Series history. I watched in disbelief as Gibby limped around the bases as the crowd went wild and the Dodgers poured out of their dugout. Describing the home run, announcer Jack Buck said, "I can't believe what I just saw!"

My sentiments exactly!

Here's another example of timing being everything. In 2005, Alan Trammell's last year as manager and my last year as a coach of the Tigers and just before the start of spring training, the team announced it had signed **Magglio Ordoñez** as a free agent with a five-year contract for a whole lot of money.

Wow! Tram and the coaches were excited about the signing. This was a guy who was a great hitter. He had hit over .300 six of his eight years with the White Sox, had driven in more than 100 runs four times, and had hit 29 or more home runs five times in the last six years. We figured we had a hitter who could single-handedly improve us by anywhere from 10 to 20 games. It was something to build on.

Magglio Ordoñez provides a powerful offensive punch on today's Tigers club.

So what happened? Ordoñez came over and in the first week of the season he strained an abdominal muscle. The strain turned out to be a hernia, and he wound up getting surgery and spending three months on the disabled list. He returned to the lineup in July and played in 82 games. He batted .302 but having missed half a season, hit only eight home runs, drove in 46 runs, and wasn't the force we thought he would be.

I have no doubt that if Ordoñez hadn't been hurt, he had played the whole season, and we had won 10 more games, a conservative number, that would have given us a record of 81–81 instead of 71-91, and Tram and his coaches might still be there today.

But that's baseball. It was just a bad break, nothing that could have been predicted and nothing that any of us—Magglio, Trammell or the coaches—could have prevented.

After Ordoñez recuperated fully, he went back to being one of the game's outstanding hitters. In 2006, he batted .298 with 24 homers and 104 RBI. In 2007, he won the American League batting title with an average of .363 (the highest by a Tiger in 70 years), hit 28 home runs, and drove in 139 runs (the most by a Tiger in 46 years). In 2008 the numbers were .317–21–103.

I wouldn't say he's a great outfielder; he's just adequate, but he *is* a great hitter. And when his career is over and it's all said and done, Magglio is going to have Hall of Fame numbers or close to them.

Statistical Summaries

All statistics are for player's Tigers career only.

HITTING

G = Games

H = Hits

HR = Home runs

RBI = Runs batted in

SB = Stolen bases

BA = Batting average

Right Fielder	Years	G	H	HR	RBI	SB	BA
Al Kaline *Doubled for his 3000th career hit in hometown of Baltimore on 9/24/74*	1953–74	2,834	3,007	399	1,583	137	.297
Harry Heilmann *Last Tiger to hit .400 (.403 in 1923)*	1914–29	1,991	2,499	164	1,442	111	.342
Sam Crawford *Missed only 33 games in 10-year period from 1906–15*	1903–17	2,114	2,466	70	1,264	317	.309

continued	Years	G	H	HR	RBI	SB	BA
Kirk Gibson *Stole three bases in 1984 World Series*	1979–86, 93–95	1,177	1,140	195	668	194	.273
Magglio Ordoñez *Has .333 career average in interleague games*	2005–09	671	807	90	442	9	.320

FIELDING

PO = Putouts

A = Assists

E = Errors

DP = Double plays

TC/G = Total chances divided by games played

FA = Fielding average

Right Fielder	PO	A	E	DP	TC/G	FA
Al Kaline	5,035	170	73	29	2.3	.986
Harry Heilmann	2,515	167	103	37	1.9	.963
Sam Crawford	2,916	197	91	44	1.7	.972
Kirk Gibson	1,688	24	43	6	2.1	.975
Magglio Ordoñez	1,027	32	16	4	1.8	.985

NINE

Right-Handed Pitcher

I debated with myself, hesitated, and deliberated a long time over making **Denny McLain** No. 1 on my all-time list of Detroit Tigers right-handed pitchers. After all, he won only 131 big-league games. Then I remembered that a lot of knowledgeable baseball people have called Sandy Koufax the greatest pitcher in the history of the game, and he won only 165. They picked Koufax because they said if they had to win one game, he's the guy they would want on the mound.

The same thing applies to Denny McLain. I know his career numbers aren't up there with guys like Jim Bunning and Jack Morris, but if I had to win one game, or better than that, if I had to have one pitcher put together a great season, I would take Denny McLain.

For a short time, McLain's numbers were amazing. In 1968, he did something that hadn't been done in 34 years, hasn't been done since, and probably will never be done again unless there's a change in the way pitchers are used—and I don't see that happening. Guys are

1.	DENNY MCLAIN
2.	JIM BUNNING
3.	JACK MORRIS
4.	TOMMY BRIDGES
5.-T	HOOKS DAUSS
5.-T	SCHOOLBOY ROWE

Although his success was short-lived, Denny McLain is the guy I'd choose on the mound to pitch the big game.

pitching less today, not more. As a result, we're never again going to see a pitcher make 41 starts, pitch 28 complete games, six shutouts, 336 innings, and win 31 games with an earned-run average of 1.96, as McLain did in '68. He was also the first American League pitcher to win both the Most Valuable Player Award and the Cy Young Award in the same season. That's pretty impressive.

In a four-year span from 1966-69, McLain won 92 games, made 157 starts, completed 75 games, and pitched 22 shutouts and 1,160⅓ innings.

Those who subscribe to the current pitching philosophy of five-man rotations and pitch counts will certainly point out that in 1970, after his spectacular four-year run, McLain had arm problems and finished with a record of 3–5, 14 starts, one complete game, and 91.1 innings pitched.
The following year he was traded to Washington, where he had a record of 10–22. He would hang on for one more season, splitting time between Oakland and Atlanta with a record of 4–7, 13 starts, two complete games, and 76⅓ innings. Then, at the age of 28, he was out of baseball.

During much of his playing career, and beyond, McLain had all kinds of off-the-field legal problems—but that doesn't take away from the career he had as a pitcher. I don't know much about him; I don't remember ever meeting him. I have heard a lot of stories about him, not all of them positive and many of them outside of his baseball career. I have also heard that he had a quick sense of humor and for that short time he was a great pitcher and competitor, the kind you'd want on the mound if you needed to win a big game.

Until some former Major League Baseball player comes along and is elected President of the United States (my money is on Derek Jeter), **Jim Bunning** is the former player who is this country's highest-ranking public servant.

Bunning is in his second term as a United States Senator from Kentucky. He also is a 17-year major league veteran who won 224 games with the Tigers, Phillies, Pirates, and Dodgers; had one 20-win season and four 19-win seasons; and was the first pitcher since Cy Young to win 100 games and strike out 1,000 batters in each league. He also is one of five to have pitched a no-hitter in each league (with the Tigers against Boston in 1958 and with the Phillies, a perfect game against the Mets in 1964). He is one of only three pitchers in the Hall of Fame who played for the Tigers, the others being Hall Newhouser and Waite Hoyt.

Now a U.S. Senator, Jim Bunning was the first pitcher since Cy Young to win 100 games and strike out 1,000 batters in both the American and National Leagues.

Bunning was a workhorse pitcher in an era filled with workhorse pitchers. He made 519 major league starts and pitched 3,760⅓ innings, 151 complete games, and 40 shutouts. Twice he made 40 or more starts in a season, twice he pitched 300 innings or more, and six times he struck out at least 200 batters. He led his league in shutouts twice, in strikeouts three times, had double figures in wins 13 times in a 14-year stretch (including 11 straight), and retired with 2,855 strikeouts (which, at the time, placed him second on the all-time list to Walter Johnson).

Unfortunately, Sen. Bunning's career is often defined by his 1964 season—the first of three straight years in which he won 19 games for the Phillies in the National League.

On September 20, he pitched a complete game, five-hit, six-strikeout, 3–2 victory over the Dodgers for his 18th win that gave the Phillies a 6½ game lead in the National League with 12 games to play. Bunning came back four days later and lost to Milwaukee. Three days after that, he again lost to Milwaukee. He came back three days later and lost to the Cardinals.

The Phillies would lose 10 straight games as Bunning and Chris Short each pitched several times with two days' rest. Bunning was the losing pitcher in three of his team's 10 straight losses and wouldn't win again until the final day of the season when he earned his 19th victory with a six-hit shutout of the Cincinnati Reds. But it was too late. The pennant had already slipped away from the Phillies.

Earlier that season, against the Mets in Shea Stadium on June 21, Bunning pitched the National League's first perfect game in 84 years. The date is significant and the outcome was appropriate. June 21, 1964, was Father's Day, and Bunning is the father of nine children.

When you talk about big-game pitchers, the name **Jack Morris** has to be part of the discussion. He was a big-game guy, someone who rose to the occasion, especially in the postseason. I can't understand why he's still not in the Hall of Fame.

Morris won 254 games, struck out 2,478 batters, was a five-time All-Star (and a three-time starter for the AL) a three-time 20-game winner, and he had a postseason record of 7–4, with 4–2 in the World Series.

What more could you want from a pitcher? Sure, he could have hung around a little longer, maybe won 300 games or struck out 3,000 batters. Either of those two things might have put him over the top and into the Hall of Fame.

Let's not dwell on what Morris did not do but concentrate on what he did:

- Led his staff in wins for 10 straight years, from 1979–88, unprecedented for a Tigers pitcher
- Led the American League in strikeouts and innings pitched and pitched into the seventh inning in 26 consecutive starts in 1983
- Pitched a no-hitter against the White Sox in 1984
- Pitched three consecutive shutouts in 1986
- Set a record for a pitcher in a five-game World Series with five putouts in 1984
- Led the American League in complete games in 1990
- Won more games in the 1980s, 162, than any other pitcher in baseball

With the Tigers, Jack is fifth all-time in wins, fourth in innings pitched, second in strikeouts and starts, and eighth in complete games and shutouts.

Sounds like a Hall of Fame résumé to me.

When Morris came into the Tigers' organization, it was obvious that he was a very good athlete. He wasn't one of those guys that only ever played baseball. Jack is from Minnesota, and I heard that he used to enjoy ski jumping, schussing down that ramp and seeing how far he could go.

Jack was always challenging himself physically, trying things just to prove that he could do them—like lying on his back and jumping to his feet like an acrobat. He was one of the guys who liked to challenge Kirk Gibson in those spring-training footraces. Once, in Toronto, Morris was feeling pretty cocky and he challenged Gibby to a race from foul pole to foul pole. Never one to turn down a challenge, Gibson said, "Let's go." So they went down to the right-field foul pole and took off across the field, but before they got halfway across, Kirk had a 20-yard lead, so Jack shut it down.

Morris' athleticism came through in his fielding. Opponents learned early in his career not to bunt on him because he covered a lot of ground, was very quick on his feet, and fielded his position very well. As a catcher, I appreciated that. It wasn't like he just threw the ball and faded out of the picture. He was always on his toes, he was always aware of situations, and he fielded his position like a fifth infielder. He helped himself out quite a bit in that regard. Despite all of that, he never won the Gold Glove—another oversight, in my opinion.

Early in his career, Morris was just a fastball/slider pitcher. When Roger Craig came to the Tigers as pitching coach, he taught Jack how to throw the split-fingered fastball, and that became his pitch—and he had a great one. He has big hands, which helped that grip considerably. He was one of the first guys with a dominant split-finger, and it became his marquee pitch. Hitters all knew he had it, but they still had a hard time hitting it.

Jack was also one of the best competitors I ever played with, on par with Kirk Gibson. They were two peas out of the same pod. Jack never wanted to come out of a game. I couldn't count the number of times Sparky Anderson went to the mound and Jack glared at him and said, "You are not taking me out of this game."

I believe Morris is the only guy who Sparky listened to when he said he wanted to stay in the game. After Jack had established himself as No. 1 on the pitching staff, more times than not he would just say, "I'm not coming out. I'm good. Let's go. Get out of here," and Sparky would get out of there and leave him in.

Hall of Fame voters should take notice—Jack Morris has put up Hall of Fame numbers!

If there is one chink in Morris' armor, it's that he threw 206 wild pitches—155 of them with Detroit, the most in Tigers history and the eighth most in baseball history. I suspect a lot of them came while he was trying to master that split-finger. It was such a new pitch and it was hard to control, just as it was hard to catch. When Jack threw the split-finger, the bottom just dropped out of it. It was there, and then suddenly it wasn't there. It increased my workload behind the plate, because most of them ended up in the dirt.

I'm not making excuses, but I wouldn't be surprised if most of the 192 passed balls I was charged with came off the split-finger.

On April 7, 1984, Morris gave me one of my biggest thrills in baseball when I caught the no-hitter he pitched against the White Sox in old Comiskey Park. It was the fourth game of the season and the first NBC *Game of the Week* that year.

It was a strange no-hitter in that Jack walked six and was in trouble in several innings, but he managed to pitch himself out of one jam after the next. He got through it, got his no-hitter, and we all ran to the mound to congratulate him. After the game and in the clubhouse, one of the attendants came over and told me that I had a phone call in the manager's office from Tigers president Jim Campbell. I couldn't figure out what the team president wanted with me, but I went in and took the call. I picked up the phone, said "Hello," and this is what I heard:

"Hey, congratulations. What a great game. You did a great job. Everybody's all excited."

He went on and on, and then he said, "There's going to be a little something extra for you in your paycheck. This was such a great achievement, we're going to put together a little bonus for you."

I was stunned, but I managed to blurt out a thanks.

Campbell continued, "When you threw that split-fingered fastball…."

"Hey, wait a minute," I said. "Who do you think you're talking to?"

"Isn't this Jack?"

"No, this is Lance."

"What the hell are you doing on the phone? Get off the phone and put Jack on."

"Okay. But is there still going to be a little something extra for me in my paycheck?"

Suffice it to say, I didn't get the bonus.

No pitcher was a Tiger longer than **Tommy Bridges**, who spent his entire 16-year major league career in Detroit. But it is not only longevity that earns Bridges the No. 4 spot among right-handed pitchers on my all-time Tigers team. He's sixth on the franchise's all-time list in wins with 194, fourth in strikeouts, fifth in complete games, third in shutouts, sixth in innings pitched,

Tommy Bridges (far right), seen here with the rest of the Tigers' 1935 pitching staff, pitched for 16 seasons, longer than any other pitcher in franchise history.

and 10th in games. He also was a six-time All-Star, a three-time 20-game winner, and the possessor of a nine-year streak of double-digit wins.

A graduate of the University of Tennessee, Bridges was supposed to follow in the footsteps of his father, who was a country doctor. Instead, the baseball bug bit him, and he signed with the Tigers, who promoted him to the big club after Bridges struck out 20 batters in one minor league game. He made his major league debut against the Yankees August 13, 1930, and the first pitch he threw in the majors was to Babe Ruth, who grounded out.

In 1934, Bridges won 22 games, helped pitch the Tigers to their first pennant in 25 years, and beat the fabled Dizzy Dean and the Cardinals 3–1 in Game 5 of the World Series. He followed that up with 21 wins in 1935 and another pennant. He beat the Cubs in the second game of the World Series and was given the ball for Game 6 with the Tigers leading the Series 3–2.

With the score tied 3–3, Stan Hack led off the top of the ninth with a triple, but Bridges stranded him by retiring the next three batters. The Tigers scored a run in the bottom of the ninth to secure their first World Series championship.

A hard thrower despite weighing between 150 and 155 pounds, Bridges led the AL in strikeouts in 1935 and '36 and four times had a no-hitter broken up in the ninth inning. On August 5, 1932, he had a perfect game against the Washington Senators with two outs in the ninth. Due to bat was the Senators' pitcher, but with the Tigers leading 13–0, Washington's manager, the immortal Walter Johnson, sent up Dave Harris, the league's leading pinch hitter.

Some said the move was poor sportsmanship on the part of Johnson, who had never pitched a perfect game. Others said it was a tribute to Johnson for honoring the integrity of the game. In any event, Harris lined a single to break up the no-hitter and the perfect game.

Bridges would finally get his no-hitter 15 years later, pitching for the Portland Beavers of the Pacific Coast League against San Francisco. He was 40 years old.

For a pitcher who won 222 games, the most in his team's history, had three 20-win seasons, and double figures in wins in 14 consecutive seasons, **George August (Hooks) Dauss** managed to fly under the radar. Although he won more games than 20 pitchers currently enshrined in the Hall of Fame, Dauss never got so much as one Hall of Fame vote.

The lack of recognition for Dauss is attributed to two factors: playing with a chronic second-division team and his easygoing demeanor.

Dauss, whose nickname derived from his assortment of tantalizing, sharp breaking balls, spent his entire 15-year major league career, from 1912–26, with the Tigers. In that 15-year period, the Tigers finished in seventh place twice, sixth place four times, and fourth place four times, with a winning percentage of .510. Dauss' winning percentage in that same period was a commendable .550.

His contemporaries believed that Dauss suffered from his friendly, good-natured personality. They reasoned that Hooks would have been an even better pitcher, perhaps a Hall of Famer, if he were a little more aggressive on the mound. Such a theory is hard to square with the fact that Dauss led the American League in hit batters three times and is the Tigers' all-time leader in hit batsmen with 121.

A mainstay during the Tigers' early years, Hooks Dauss has been largely undervalued.

Look, out on the mound. It's a bird! It's a plane! It's Superman! No, it's a bird by the name of Mark "the Bird" Fidrych, one of the most colorful characters not only in the history of the Tigers but in all of baseball. He was a gangly kid of 21, all arms and legs, and he pranced around the mound and did quirky, kooky things. He talked to the baseball, he got down on all fours and smoothed the dirt on the mound. If a Tigers infielder helped him by making an outstanding play, he would walk to his teammate's position and shake his hand.

Fidrych's career took off like a meteor and, because of arm problems, it descended just as rapidly.

Orioles manager Earl Weaver: "I was sitting in my office one night after a game, and Pat Santarone, our groundskeeper, came running in. He had the Detroit game on television, and he said, 'I seen the damnedest thing I've ever seen. There's a pitcher that's talking to the ball.'

"I said, 'What are you talking about?'

"He said, 'He gets down on the mound and he does everything and he talks to the ball.'

"They pitched him in Baltimore, and we never filled that park all the time in Memorial Stadium, but when the Tigers came in and they announced he was pitching, we had 45,000 in the place.

"It was funny, but the guy won. He was a winner. The strange thing about it was the ballplayers didn't get mad. When you're winning and he keeps getting you out, a guy like Frank Robinson is going to say something nasty. The guy talks to the ball and then gets Frank out. Frank woulda went nuts, I think. But [Fidrych] just entertained everybody."

Tigers manager Ralph Houk: "I don't think he really talked to the ball. He talked to himself. But if they wanted to say he talked to the ball, that's great. My pitching coach, Fred Gladding, had seen him pitch in the minor leagues, and he said, 'Don't pay attention to all that stuff he does out there. This kid can pitch.'

"Every time I used him that spring [1976] he got hitters out. The thing that made him was the game he pitched against the Yankees in Tiger Stadium [before a national television audience on the *Game of the Week*, Monday, June 28, a 5–1 Tigers victory for Fidrych's eighth win in nine decisions].

"We'd go on the road, and I'd have general managers calling me and saying, 'You've got to pitch him here.' I tried to make out the rotation the best I could so that he'd pitch in Detroit so our fans could see him. I'd get calls, he hasn't pitched here and he hasn't pitched there, and everywhere we went and he pitched, he'd pack the place."

Fidrych: "I got the name ['the Bird'] from Jeff Hogan, who was my coach when I broke in with Bristol, Virginia, in the Appalachian Rookie League. He said I reminded him of Big Bird from Sesame Street.

"The things I did on the mound, I always did. My dad told me about filling the holes on the mound so if the ball was hit back to me, I wouldn't get a bad hop, or if I stepped, I wouldn't land in a hole. When I was a kid, I used to talk a lot when I was pitching, like, 'OK, throw a strike,' the same as you see some hitters talk to themselves about keeping their head down, keeping their shoulder in, or keeping their eye on the ball.

"When I got to the Tigers, my pitching coach, Fred Gladding, told me to keep doing what I was doing. He said if I changed my ways, I might not be there. Ralph Houk just let me be myself.

"Everywhere I went, the other team tried to do something to distract me. In Cleveland, they threw birdseed on the pitcher's mound. Another time, somebody threw me a ball that had writing all over it. In Minnesota, when I was going for my 13th win, they released 13 pigeons around home plate. I didn't mind. It was part of the game. The way I looked at it, they were having their fun and I was having mine."

Rusty Staub: "The first time I saw Mark Fidrych was in spring training. He was a pretty high-strung kid that I don't think anybody really thought was going to make the big leagues that year. He looked extremely good in spring training, and the one thing that stood out is that he always kept the ball down. And he seemed to have good control.

"When spring training was over, he made the club. The antics were real. The biggest thing about Fidrych is that all those things he did, he did all the time. He talked to the ball, he talked to the ground, he talked to the sky. I mean he talked to everything. He would fidget on the mound, and he'd go to the back of the mound and pick up mud and rub it on his hands.

"Things like that were a little bit awkward for people who may have seen major league baseball and how professional it can be, but it was so real. In Detroit, no one had ever seen anything like that. I don't think anybody had ever seen this anywhere.

"It was electrifying for me to watch what happened to him, the way he excited people. I appreciated something that was new and great in the game that I hadn't seen in a while. I saw Sandy Koufax. When Vida Blue came up, he was pretty exciting. But nothing like this guy. There was nobody like Fidrych. I can only tell you that when he did his thing, the fans went crazy."

Although he didn't make his first start until the 1976 season was a month old, Fidrych won 19 games and lost nine for a team that was 13 games under .500. He led the American League with an earned-run average of 2.34 and in complete games with 24 and was named American League Rookie of the Year.

The next spring, he tore cartilage on his left knee. Later, he hurt his arm. He would pitch four more seasons for the Tigers, winning 10 and losing 10. He tried several comebacks, the last in 1983, when he pitched for Pawtucket in the International League. In midseason, with a record of 2–5 and an ERA of 9.68, Mark Fidrych retired for good. The Bird was 28 years old.

Although his career record cannot measure up to Hooks Dauss', I've selected **Lynwood "Schoolboy" Rowe** in a tie for fifth place on my all-time list of Tigers right-handed pitchers—partly because of his career, which started out so spectacularly, was unfortunately shortened by injury, and partly because he had one of the greatest nicknames in baseball history and was one of the most engaging characters of his time.

He became "Schoolboy" Rowe when, as a 15-year-old high school student, he played with a men's sandlot team in his native Texas. The name stuck with him until his dying day.

Rowe's career started out like he was skyrocketing straight for the Hall of Fame. In 1932 he led the Texas League in wins and ERA, earning him a promotion to Detroit the following season. Used sparingly, he appeared in 19 games for the Tigers, winning seven and losing four. The following year, he hit it big with a mark of 24–8, including an American League–record 16 consecutive wins, helping the Tigers to the pennant.

In the second game of the 1934 World Series against the St. Louis Cardinals' "Gashouse Gang," Schoolboy went the distance and beat the Cardinals 3–2 in 12 innings. He came back in Game 6 and again went the distance but lost to Paul Dean 4–3. In 1935 Rowe followed up with 19 wins, and the Tigers won their second straight pennant. Schoolboy lost Game 1 of the World Series to the Cubs 3–0, came back two days later with four innings of relief to win Game 3, but lost Game 5 3–1.

In addition to his outstanding pitching, Schoolboy was one of the best hitting pitchers ever. Playing in an era when American League pitchers batted, he was a force offensively, batting .303 with eight doubles, two home

Perhaps better known for his hitting, Schoolboy Rowe (far right) was also a terrific pitcher who paid dividends to the Tigers, among other major league teams. Here, the star pitcher poses before Game 1 of the 1934 World Series with his manager Mickey Cochrane, Cardinals manager Frankie Frisch, pitcher Dizzy Dean, and his eminence, Babe Ruth.

runs, and 22 RBI in 1934, and .312 with three home runs and 28 RBI in 1935. Rowe had a career average of .263 with 18 home runs and 153 RBI.

When he won 19 games again in 1936, it made 69 games in four seasons. At age 26, he seemed on the fast track to Cooperstown. But the wear and tear of having pitched almost 800 innings over three seasons took its toll. In the next two seasons, he would be limited to 52 innings, would win only one game, and be returned to the minor leagues. He came back to win 10 games in 1939 and to lead the American League in winning percentage in 1940 when he was 16–3 and again helped the Tigers win another pennant. But the following season he slipped to 8–6 and his days in Detroit were coming to an end.

On April 30 he was sold to the Brooklyn Dodgers, ending one of the most colorful chapters in Detroit baseball. Rowe was fiercely superstitious. He carried talismans and charms in his uniform pockets, always picked up his glove with his left hand, and predated Mark "the Bird" Fidrych by talking to the baseball.

Once, during the Tigers' run to the 1934 pennant, Schoolboy appeared as a guest on the popular Eddie Cantor national radio program. Rowe had recently become engaged to his high school sweetheart, Edna Mary Skinner, who was listening back home in Texas. At one point, as the host was interviewing Rowe, Schoolboy blurted out, "How'm I doing, Edna, honey?"

It wasn't long before the line was repeated frequently by Cantor on his weekly show or for fans and opposing players to taunt Schoolboy with the words, "How'm I doing, Edna?"

The risk of taking on a project like this is that there's a very good chance of omitting some players on an all-time team who deserve to be included. I readily admit that I may have done some players a disservice, especially those who played long before I was born and about whom there is very little information except for career statistics.

I was able to find out some things about Hooks Dauss, but another pitcher I know little about is George Mullin, who pitched for the Tigers from 1902–13. Does he deserve to be rated among the top five right-handed pitchers in Tigers history? Should he be rated ahead of Denny McLain? Jack Morris? Tommy Bridges? I really don't know.

The man did win 209 games as a Tiger, second on their all-time list, and he pitched 34 shutouts, also second among Tigers. He won more than 20 games five times and was in double figures in victories in each of his 11 full seasons with the Tigers.

But he pitched in the dead-ball era when pitchers often started with two and sometimes even one day of rest. In the four-year period from 1904–07, Mullin started 167 games and pitched in relief eight times.

He lost 20 games or more three times and was in double figures in losses 10 of his 11 years in Detroit. Although his 209 wins as a Tiger are impressive, it's difficult to ignore the 179 losses that went along with them.

While I'm putting in my disclaimer for George Mullin, I should also mention these other Tigers right-handed pitchers who merited serious consideration for my list—Dizzy Trout, Virgil "Fire" Trucks, Frank Lary, famed Yankee killer Earl Wilson, "Wild Bill" Donovan, and current ace Justin Verlander, who one day may force himself into the top five.

Statistical Summaries

All statistics are for player's Tigers career only.

PITCHING

G = Games
W = Games won
L = Games lost
PCT = Winning percentage
SHO = Shutouts
SO = Strikeouts
ERA = Earned-run average

Right-Handed Pitcher	Years	G	W	L	PCT	SHO	SO	ERA
Denny McLain *Led league in home runs allowed three consecutive seasons (1966–68)*	1963–70	227	11/	62	.654	26	1,150	3.13
Jim Bunning *Struck out the side on nine pitches vs. Boston, 8/2/59*	1955–63	304	118	87	.576	16	1,406	3.45
Jack Morris *Had 32–12 career record vs. Cleveland*	1977–90	430	198	150	.569	24	1,086	3.73

continued	Years	G	W	L	PCT	SHO	SO	ERA
Tommy Bridges *Defeated St. Louis Browns on 8/23/30 despite walking 12 batters*	1930–43, 1945–46	424	194	138	.584	33	1,674	3.57
Hooks Dauss *Won 21 games in 1919, lost 21 games the following season*	1912-26	538	222	182	.550	22	1,201	3.30
Schoolboy Rowe *Batted combined .307 with five homers and 50 RBI in 1934 and '35*	1933-42	245	105	62	.629	16	662	4.01

FIELDING

PO = Putouts

A = Assists

E = Errors

DP = Double plays

TC/G = Total chances divided by games played

FA = Fielding average

Right-Handed Pitcher	PO	A	E	DP	TC/G	FA
Denny McLain	125	176	12	14	1.4	.962
Jim Bunning	105	163	8	10	0.9	.971
Jack Morris	321	333	22	31	1.6	.967
Tommy Bridges	144	469	24	23	1.5	.962
Hooks Dauss	99	1,128	41	25	2.4	.968
Schoolboy Rowe	66	272	8	17	1.4	.977

TEN

Left-Handed Pitcher

Twenty pitchers have won the Most Valuable Player Award. Of those 20 pitchers, three have won it twice. But only one pitcher has won back-to-back Most Valuable Player Awards. His name is **Hal Newhouser**, and he pitched for the Tigers from 1939 to '53.

The Cy Young Award originated in 1956, so prior to that time pitchers were judged along with position players in the MVP voting. Newhouser won his first American League MVP in 1944 when he was one victory short of being the first pitcher in 10 years to win 30 games, posting a record of 29–9. He had two saves, an earned-run average of 2.22, 25 complete games in 34 starts, six shutouts, 312⅓ innings, and he led the league in strikeouts with 187.

1.	HAL NEWHOUSER
2.	MICKEY LOLICH
3.	HARRY COVELESKI
4.	FRANK TANANA
5.	HANK AGUIRRE

A year later, he won the MVP again with a record of 25–9, leading the league in wins, ERA (1.81), starts (36), complete games (29), shutouts (8), strikeouts (212), and innings (313⅓). He led the Tigers to the American League pennant and pitched two

Hal Newhouser carries the distinction of being the only pitcher to have won consecutive MVP awards.

complete game victories over the Cubs in the World Series, including the Game 7 clincher.

In 1946 Newhouser again led the league in wins with 26 (he lost 9), and ERA (1.94). He also pitched six shutouts, worked 292⅔ innings, and struck out 275 batters. But he was second in the American League to Bob Feller, who struck out 348. Newhouser might have won a third consecutive Most Valuable Player Award were it not for the mighty Ted Williams, who batted .342, hit 38 home runs, and drove in 123 runs; Williams was voted MVP by 27 points over Newhouser, the runner-up.

Newhouser is another Tiger who was a Detroit native. In 1939, at age 18, he signed out of high school with his hometown team for a bonus of $400. Legend has it that only minutes after signing, a Cleveland Indians scout arrived with an offer of a $15,000 bonus plus a new car, but the deal with the Tigers was already done.

The young lefthander pitched in 34 minor league games in 1939, came up at the end of the season to make one start for the Tigers, and never returned to the minors. Newhouser would struggle over the next five seasons, winning 34 games and losing 51. But in 1944 he had his breakout season, winning 29 games and the American League Most Valuable Player Award. It was the beginning of a three-year run as the most dominant pitcher in baseball, in which he won 80 games and lost only 27.

After slipping to a record of 17–17 in 1947, Newhouser bounced back in 1948 with the fourth 20-win season of his career and a record of 21–12. In the 1940s, Newhouser and Feller were regarded as the two most dominant pitchers in the American League, and their head-to-head confrontations were instant classics.

On September 22, 1946, Newhouser beat Feller 3–0, but then Feller turned the tables and reeled off five consecutive wins in *mano a mano* battles with Newhouser. They would meet again in Cleveland on the final day of the 1948 season with Feller's Indians one game ahead of the Red Sox.

Newhouser got his revenge on Feller with a complete game, five-hit, 7–1 victory, barely losing his shutout in the bottom of the ninth. Meanwhile, in New York, the Red Sox blasted the Yankees 10–5, throwing the final standings into a tie between the Indians and Red Sox and forcing a one-game playoff to determine the American League champion. Luckily for Feller and the Indians, they would go on to win the playoff and ultimately the World Series.

The scene: Tigertown in Lakeland, Florida. Spring training 1975.

I had been invited to big-league camp mainly because I was a catcher and catchers are always needed in the early part of spring training. I was just a 19-year-old kid with 68 games in a rookie league under my belt, trying to make an impression with the Tigers and willing to do anything asked of me just to draw attention to myself.

Part of my job was to warm up pitchers in the bullpen, so I was hyped up not only about being in big-league camp but also to catch all those big-league pitchers. One of them was **Mickey Lolich**, a grizzled old veteran, all of 34 years old, who had won almost 200 major league games and had been the star of the Tigers' 1968 World Series championship.

Tigertown is situated on an old military base, and there are airplane hangars on the grounds. One of the hangars was converted into a workout facility replete with several pitching mounds and a batting cage. When it rained, the players would go to the hangar to work out.

One day I was inside the hangar catching Lolich, and he told me he wanted to throw some knuckleballs. I don't know if he ever used it in games, but he had a pretty good knuckleball and loved to toy with it in the bullpen. I'm thinking, *That's great, just what I need, trying to catch Lolich's knuckleball. I'm liable to end up with a broken finger.* But who am I to tell the great Mickey Lolich what to do? So I gave him a lukewarm "Okay," and steeled myself to catch his knuckleball.

He must have thrown me 10 of those knuckleballs, and I don't think I got a glove on one of them. He just beat me to death with them. They hit me everywhere but my glove. After the first three or four, the pitching coach walked over and Mickey said something to him, and the two of them looked over at me and started chuckling. That's when I knew that I had been set up.

Lolich would throw a knuckleball and, bam! He hit me in the forearm. Bam! He hit me in the mask. Mickey and the coach were laughing, but to me, it really wasn't that funny. It did give me an idea of how good a pitcher Lolich was. From his display, I concluded that he could have been a knuckleball pitcher. I was thinking, *Who the heck could hit that?*

The most interesting thing about Lolich is that he did everything right-handed—eat, write, even throw a baseball—until he broke his left collarbone in a childhood accident. Rehabbing his left arm made it stronger than his right, so when he started playing baseball he found he could throw the ball

Mickey Lolich is one of only a handful of pitchers to win three games in a World Series. He did it in 1968 against the St. Louis Cardinals, winning the decisive seventh game on only two days' rest.

harder with his left hand. In fact, he threw so hard and was such a good pitcher at a young age that the Tigers signed him out of high school.

After spending four years and part of a fifth in the minor leagues, Lolich landed in Detroit to stay in 1963, the same year Dennis McLain arrived. They would give the Tigers a one-two pitching punch, combining to win 125 games over the next five seasons before hitting it big in 1968, when McLain won 31 and Lolich won 17 en route to the American League pennant. The Tigers won 103 games and finished 12 games in front of Baltimore in the American League that year and then took on the St. Louis Cardinals in the World Series.

It was "the Year of the Pitcher," and there were many choices if one was looking for a pitcher to be the Most Valuable Player of the World Series. Would it be McLain, a 31-game winner, or Bob Gibson, who won 22 games, pitched 13 shutouts, and had a miniscule earned-run average of 1.12?

Would it be 19-game winner Nelson Briles, fire-balling left-hander Steve Carlton, or John Hiller, the Tigers' lockdown closer?

It turned out to be none of the above. The star of the 1968 World Series was Lolich, the portly left-hander, who won Game 2 8–1 on a complete game six-hitter and even hit a home run in the third inning (it would be his only home run in 840 regular-season and postseason at-bats). He came back four days later with another complete game to win Game 5 5–3 and returned on two days' rest in Game 7 to beat Gibson 4–1 with another complete game.

People always got on Lolich because he was overweight and they worried that his weight was putting too much of a strain on his arm. I guess he was the David Wells and CC Sabathia of his day, but he was a model of consistency as well as a workhorse in his years with the Tigers. People say he had a rubber arm. He could throw and throw and throw. He won 14 or more games for 11 straight seasons and made at least 30 starts for 12 consecutive seasons. In a four-year span from 1971–74, after McLain was gone and Lolich was the Tigers' ace, he averaged 20 wins, 42 starts, 24 complete games, 330 innings, and 244 strikeouts season. In 1971, he led the American League in wins (25), complete games (29), innings (376), and strikeouts (308).

When he retired, Lolich was baseball's all-time strikeout leader among lefthanders (he has since been passed by Randy Johnson and Steve Carlton). He also is No. 1 on the Tigers' all-time list in strikeouts, shutouts, and starts and No. 3 in wins and innings.

Mickey is a great representative of the Tigers. He's a regular at their fantasy camps, and the fans all love him. It's no wonder! He had a great career. He rose to the occasion and he endeared himself to Tigers fans forever by what he did in the '68 World Series.

Not to be confused with his younger, more famous and more successful brother Stan, a right-hander, **Harry Coveleski** was left-handed and packed most of his major league career into five memorable days in 1908 and three consecutive 20-win seasons in the middle of the 20th century's second decade.

Harry "the Giant Killer" Coveleski (left) showed flashes of brilliance, but it was his brother Stanley (right) who would go on to a Hall of Fame career.

A native Pennsylvanian, Coveleski signed with the Philadelphia Phillies in 1907 at age 21 and appeared in four games for the Phillies late that season. He was sent back to the minor leagues the following year. Once again he was a September call-up, and this time he made a strong impression by beating the New York Giants three times in a five-day period.

On September 29, he shut out the Giants 7–0. Two days later, he again beat the Giants 6–2, and two days after that he beat them again, 3–2. Teammates and writers tabbed him "the Giant Killer," a nickname that stayed with him for his entire career.

When he won only six games and lost 10 in 1909, Coveleski was traded to Cincinnati, where he appeared in only seven games and won one (in one game he walked 16 batters). He was sent back down to the minors and spent the next three years honing his craft until the Tigers purchased his contract and brought him to Detroit.

Over the next three seasons, Coveleski won 65 games—22 each in 1914 and '15 and 21 in 1916. Only the great Walter Johnson won more games in the American League over that three-year span.

At the time, Harry had a major league record of 77–48, and his brother Stan, coming along behind him, had a record of 17–14. But Harry would win only four more major league games before fading out of sight, while Stan, "the Other Coveleski," would win 198 more games, have five 20-win seasons, finish with a career mark of 215–142, and be elected to the Hall of Fame.

Harry never came close to reaching his kid brother's success, but he left his mark in Detroit. In four of his five seasons with the Tigers, he had an earned-run average under three runs per game, and his 2.34 ERA as a Tiger is still the all-time franchise career record.

I hit against **Frank Tanana** when he was with the Angels, and I caught him when he came to the Tigers—and you would never know it was the same pitcher. Talk about a pitcher reinventing himself! That was Tanana.

When he was young, Tanana could throw as hard as anybody. When he came up with the California Angels in 1973, Nolan Ryan was already there, and they became some dominant one-two punch. The slogan was "Tanana and Ryan and Two Days of Cryin'" but after those two, the Angels didn't have very much to brag about. You could go into Anaheim for a couple of

No hitter wanted to face
Frank Tanana; he had
great stuff at any speed.

games, and if you had to face those two guys back-to-back, they could put you in a slump in a hurry. In 1976, they combined for 36 wins, nine shutouts, and 588 strikeouts.

I have talked to baseball people who have said that in Anaheim at that time, Tanana, not Ryan, was "the man." And you have to be something special if you're "the man" on a pitching staff that includes Nolan Ryan.

One guy said, "I would rather face Nolan Ryan than Frank Tanana." That surprised me at first, but I soon came to understand it. At the time, Tanana threw every bit as hard as Ryan, and he wasn't afraid to run one up under your chin when he had to. He intimidated hitters and overpowered them. Everybody thought highly of his ability. They weren't putting radar guns on pitchers in those days, but the word was Tanana could bring it better than 100 mph.

He certainly was held in high esteem and was a very dominant guy as far as "stuff" went, but his record didn't reflect that sort of thing. He never won 20 games, though he did win 18 and 19, led the league in strikeouts in 1975, ERA in 1977, and had one game with 17 strikeouts.

When Tanana came to the Tigers in 1985 and I got a chance to catch him, he was a completely different pitcher. He had hurt his arm and couldn't throw 100 mph anymore, so he had to come up with something different. He developed an assortment of off-speed pitches—and he was just as successful as he had been when he threw 100 mph.

Tanana had double figures in wins in seven of his eight years with the Tigers (he won nine games in the other year). This guy was a magician on the mound. He amazed me. He could throw any pitch anywhere, at any speed, and throw it for a strike. He would just pick, pick, pick you to death.

Tanana could tie a hitter up in knots. He'd throw that big, slow curveball and then he'd take a little more off and throw it again, slower than before. Then he'd buzz you with a fastball inside that was maybe 88 mph but seemed like the mid-90s to hitters lulled to sleep by all that slow stuff. If you were hitting against him, you'd be trying to stay back, stay back, and not lunge at his slow stuff...and then he'd stand you up by buzzing his fastball up and in.

He'd pick the inside corner with his fastball, and when you were looking for the ball inside, he'd turn it over against right-handed hitters and clip the outside corner. They called him "the Great Tantalizer" because he drove hitters crazy. I enjoyed working with him as much as any pitcher I ever caught. It was fun for me to try to get on the same page as him. I tried to think along with him. I'd ask myself, "What would he want to throw here?" I did that because I respected his intelligence as a pitcher. He knew how to pitch, and he knew how to set guys up—things he never really had to do when he was just a thrower.

There was one game against the Yankees in which Frank had the hitters going crazy. He'd put a little on, take a little off. One of the Yankees, I don't remember who, struck out, took one step out of the batter's box toward the dugout, stopped, looked out at the mound, and screamed at the top of his voice, "GO BACK AND WARM UP!"

164

*C*alled up from Indianapolis of the American Association by the Cleveland Indians, 24-year-old Hank Aguirre made his major league debut September 10, 1955, in Boston's Fenway Park, brought in by manager Al Lopez to pitch the sixth inning against the Red Sox.

Aguirre retired Billy Goodman on a line drive to shortstop George Strickland, got Billy Klaus to roll over a ground ball to second baseman Bobby Avila, who threw to first baseman Al Rosen for the out, and then faced the redoubtable Ted Williams, 36 years old at the time but still a force at the plate, winding down a season in which he would bat .356, hit 28 home runs, and drive in 83 runs. Aguirre struck him out.

What happened after that may be apocryphal, but considering the principals, is highly credible and, nonetheless, worth retelling.

Aware, and in awe, of Williams' status in major league baseball, Aguirre, who had retrieved the baseball after the strikeout, approached Williams after the game and asked him to autograph the baseball. Williams, by then a full-fledged curmudgeon and always an egotist when it came to his hitting prowess, at first was reluctant to indulge Aguirre's request. Finally, he relented and handed over to Aguirre his prized souvenir.

Some years later, Aguirre again faced Williams, now nearing his retirement but still a potent batting force. Aguirre wound up and delivered, Williams swung, and the baseball disappeared out of sight.

As he circled the bases, Williams looked out on the mound and shouted at Aguirre, "Get that ball and I'll sign that one, too."

I never caught **Hank Aguirre**, but I knew him. He came around during spring training, and I ran into him at Tigers functions like fantasy camps. As much fun as Frank Tanana was to catch, Hank Aguirre was fun to be around. He had a terrific sense of humor, and he always seemed to come up with a one-liner that would break everybody up. Hank was a great storyteller and a big jokester. Even when he wasn't around, if his name came up in the conversation, there was a ready story to be told about Hank and his exploits.

His batting average was terrible, but Hank Aguirre was a terrific pitcher and a great guy to be around.

Guys used to like to get on him about his hitting, and he would join in the fun. He had a lifetime batting average of .085 and batted under .040 in seven of his 16 seasons. All of that ribbing was in good fun and was certainly deserved. But what is undeserved and grossly unfair is that Hank has never been given his due as a pitcher.

For most of his career, Aguirre was used in relief. He came up with Cleveland in 1955 and was traded to the Tigers in 1958. By 1962, he had been in the major leagues for seven seasons, had started only 20 games, and had never pitched as many as 100 innings in any season.

On May 26, 1962, the Tigers were scheduled to play the Yankees at Yankee Stadium. Detroit manager Bob Scheffing had planned to start Don Mossi, but Mossi came up with a sore arm. Preferring lefthanders in Yankee Stadium, Scheffing gave the ball to Aguirre, who had not started a game all season.

When he came through with a complete game, five-hit, 2–1 victory over the Yankees, Aguirre was put in the starting rotation for the remainder of the year. He finished the season with a 16–8 record and an earned-run average of 2.21, the best in the major leagues and the lowest for a Tigers pitcher since Hal Newhouser 16 years earlier.

Over the next three seasons, used almost exclusively as a starter, Aguirre won 49 games. But in 1966 he was returned to the bullpen. He finished his career three games over .500 with an ERA of 3.24. You can bet there are a lot of guys pitching in the big leagues today who would like to have a 3.24 ERA.

Statistical Summaries

All statistics are for player's Tigers career only.

PITCHING

G = Games

W = Games won

L = Games lost

PCT = Winning percentage

SHO = Shutouts

SO = Strikeouts

ERA = Earned-run average

Left-Handed Pitcher	Years	G	W	L	PCT	SHO	SO	ERA
Hal Newhouser *Triple Crown winner in 1945, led league in wins (25), strikeouts (212) and ERA (1.81)*	1939–53	460	200	148	.575	33	1,770	3.07
Mickey Lolich *Pitched more than 300 innings four consecutive seasons (1971–74)*	1963–75	508	207	175	.542	39	2,679	3.45
Harry Coveleski *Led league with 50 pitching appearances in 1915*	1914–18	157	69	43	.616	9	400	2.34

continued	Years	G	W	L	PCT	SHO	SO	ERA
Frank Tanana *Pitched 1–0 shutout vs. Toronto to clinch division title on final day of 1987 season*	1985–92	250	96	82	.539	7	958	4.08
Hank Aguirre *Pitched three innings in second 1962 All-Star Game*	1958–67	334	64	64	.500	7	755	3.29

FIELDING

PO = Putouts

A = Assists

E = Errors

DP = Double plays

TC/G = Total chances divided by games played

FA = Fielding average

Left-Handed Pitcher	PO	A	E	DP	TC/G	FA
Hal Newhouser	132	604	22	40	1.6	.971
Mickey Lolich	90	406	32	15	1.0	.939
Harry Coveleski	36	387	25	15	2.9	.967
Frank Tanana	98	246	6	18	1.4	.983
Hank Aguirre	41	138	20	5	0.6	.899

ELEVEN

Relief Pitcher

Considering the physical problem he had to overcome and the era in which he pitched, **John Hiller** should be regarded among the elite relief pitchers in baseball history. But he will never get the recognition he deserves because he saved more than 15 games in a season only once and in 15 seasons accumulated only 125 saves, or less than 10 per season. Almost 100 relievers have saved more.

If Hiller pitched under today's conditions, when closers are called in to a game in the ninth inning with a lead of three runs or less, he could easily have had at least 100 more career saves.

In 1973, when Hiller had his big year with 38 saves in 65 appearances, a 1.44 earned-run average, and 125⅓ innings for an average of 1.92 innings per appearance, the Tigers had 39 complete games. In 2008, they had one. In '73, in addition to his 38 saves, Hiller won 10 games. In 2008, no relief pitcher won more than eight games.

To put it briefly: Times, and the role of the relief pitcher, have changed.

1. JOHN HILLER

2. WILLIE HERNANDEZ

3. TODD JONES

4. MIKE HENNEMAN

5. AURELIO LOPEZ

In 1971, John Hiller suffered a debilitating stroke and heart attack. Two years later he nabbed 38 saves and Comeback Player of the Year honors.

These days, pitchers are groomed as specialists in the minor leagues, in college, in high school, and, I suspect, even in Little League. That wasn't the case in John Hiller's day.

A native of Scarborough, Ontario, a suburb of Toronto, John was signed by the Tigers in June 1962 and began his professional career the following spring in Jamestown, New York. In his first two minor league seasons, he shifted between starting and relieving. It wasn't until his third year, with Montgomery in the Southern League, that the Tigers began grooming John as a reliever. Yet when he reached Detroit to stay in 1967, the Tigers still had not made up their minds on how they wanted to use him. Hiller spent his first four big-league seasons switching from starter to reliever and back again with moderate success.

By 1970, Hiller had become a reliever almost exclusively. He made only five starts in 47 games and had a record of 6–6 and three saves. And then tragedy struck. On January 11, 1971, at the age of 27, Hiller was felled by a massive stroke and heart attack that nearly took his life. He endured a lengthy recovery and, because the Tigers had such a high regard for him, they invited him to their 1972 spring training camp to serve as a coach and batting practice pitcher, though they had no thought of Hiller resuming his career.

But John had other ideas. By May, he was throwing as well as he had before his heart attack. His doctors gave him full clearance to attempt a comeback.

Hiller was returned to the roster in July and became an important part of the Tigers' run to the American League East title, appearing in 24 games, including three starts, with one win, three saves, and a 2.04 earned-run average. His only win came in an important start on the final weekend of the season, a complete game 5–1 victory over the Milwaukee Brewers.

Hiller's big year came a year later when, pitching exclusively in relief, his 38 saves set a major league record that would last for 10 years and a Tigers record that would last for 27 years. He was named baseball's Comeback Player of the Year and American League Fireman of the Year; was fourth in the American League Cy Young voting behind Jim Palmer, Nolan Ryan, and Catfish Hunter, all 20-game winners; and tied with Rod Carew and Sal Bando for fourth in the Most Valuable Player voting behind Reggie Jackson, Palmer, and Amos Otis.

The following year, again pitching exclusively in relief, his saves dropped to 13, but he won 17 games, breaking Dick Radatz's American League record for most wins in relief.

I didn't catch up with John until he was in the last few years of his career. I was just a kid, still learning how to catch, when he paid me a nice compliment that I will never forget and will always appreciate. He was quoted in the newspapers saying that he thought I did a good job behind the plate and that he enjoyed throwing to me. That made me feel great, that I had come a long way in my catching when a veteran pitcher like Hiller paid me such a high compliment.

Hiller was a fastball, breaking ball, change-up guy. If the split-finger was the equalizer for Jack Morris, for John it was his change-up. He had a great one. He would throw it at any time, on any count, to any hitter, in any situation.

One of the things I liked best about Hiller as a pitcher is that he tried to make things as uncomplicated as possible. Working with him was easy. If I signaled for a fastball and he wanted to throw a change-up, he just threw a change-up. Because a change-up is on the same plane as a fastball, only slower, he could do that and it wouldn't cross me up. He had the freedom to do it and I was comfortable with him doing it, so it made the signal calling go more quickly. Every once in a while he would mix in a breaking ball, but he spotted his fastball very well and threw that change-up whenever he wanted to. He was fun for me to catch. I regret that he wasn't around longer after I got there.

Hiller retired after the 1980 season with 125 saves, at the time fourth on the American League's all-time list and first on the Tigers' all-time list. It was a record he held for 13 years. He's one of a handful of players who spent their entire major league career with the Tigers. His comeback and his courage in overcoming adversity is one of baseball's most inspirational stories.

Similar to John Hiller, **Willie Hernandez** was a pitcher who pretty much bordered on mediocrity, shifting between starting and relieving, until he had one big breakout year. Willie's came in 1984, his first season with the Tigers after having spent seven years in the National League, mostly with the Cubs.

Hernandez was signed by the Phillies and picked up by the Cubs in the Rule 5 draft. Used mostly in relief, Hernandez won 16 games and saved seven in his first two years in Chicago. After a 4–4 season in '79, the Cubs tried him as a starter the following year, but he failed miserably and was returned to the bullpen.

A screwball pitcher, Willie Hernandez is one of the Tigers' top five in saves—including this big one to win 1984 World Series, which he and I are celebrating here.

After two more mediocre seasons, Willie was traded back to the Phillies, and it was there that he resurrected his career. He won eight games and saved seven and was traded to the Tigers with Dave Bergman in exchange for Glenn Wilson and John Wockenfuss. It turned out to be one of the Tigers' best trades.

In his first season with us Willie appeared in a league-high 80 games and was 9–3 with a 1.92 earned-run average and 32 saves for our American League championship team. He also saved one game in the American League Championship Series and two in the World Series. He was money in the bank that year, about as consistent as any pitcher I've ever caught. He was fairly automatic. When he came into a game, he almost always got the job done.

As great a season as Hernandez had in 1984, it was no better than John Hiller's in '73. Although Hiller finished fourth in both the Most Valuable Player and Cy Young voting, Hernandez won both of those prestigious awards. He beat out Kent Hrbek, Dan Quisenberry, and Eddie Murray for the MVP and finished ahead of Quisenberry and Bert Blyleven for the Cy Young.

Hernandez followed up his huge year with two more big ones, eight wins and 31 saves in 1985, and eight wins and 24 saves in 1986, giving him a three-year total of 25 wins and 87 saves before he went into decline.

Willie's signature pitch was the screwball, although he also had a fastball, curveball, and slider. He had so many pitches, you'd run out of fingers with him. He would also occasionally drop down and throw sidearm to try to change the look and the angle and be more effective against left-handed hitters.

Willie ended up with 147 saves in his career—120 of them for the Tigers, making him fourth on their all-time list.

When I think of the much-traveled **Todd Jones** (he pitched for 16 seasons with eight different major league teams, including two separate tours with the Tigers) I'm reminded of a relief pitcher named Don Stanhouse, who closed games for the Orioles in the 1970s. Baltimore manager Earl Weaver used to call Stanhouse "Full Pack."

Weaver practically chain-smoked cigarettes in those days, and he used to sneak down in the runway of the dugout for a quick smoke during games.

The more tense the situation, the more Earl smoked. Stanhouse would come in to save games in the eighth or ninth inning, and invariably it seemed like he would put runners on base and make a tense situation even more tense. So he called Stanhouse "Full Pack," because Earl often went through a full pack of cigarettes watching Stanhouse pitch in and out of trouble. Jones was the same kind of exasperating reliever.

Todd began his career with the Houston Astros, where he was used mostly as a set-up man. He came to Detroit in a big, nine-player trade in 1997 and had his best years with the Tigers, who made him their closer. In six years during his first tenure with the Tigers, he saved 142 games.

I worked with Todd in 2000 when I was coaching in Detroit; he led the American League that year with 42 saves. He had a good fastball and a good breaking ball, but, like Stanhouse, he got himself into plenty of jams, as his 3.52 ERA attests. Nothing ever went smoothly for Todd. He'd drive you crazy. He'd put runners on base and constantly walk a tightrope. He'd always

Todd Jones was a successful reliever—but it always seemed that he got through by the skin of his teeth.

be in trouble, but he had the ability to pitch himself out of the jams he created.

After leaving the Tigers, Todd bounced around to the Twins, the Rockies, the Red Sox, the Reds, the Phillies, and the Marlins before coming back to the Tigers in 2006. A year later, he became the 21st reliever in baseball history to compile 300 saves.

He finished his career with 319 saves (and an earned-run average of 3.97) and as the Tigers' all-time save leader with 235. His total saves don't necessarily tell the story of how Todd got there, however. He was a product of his times. He pitched in an era when closers were used differently and got more opportunities for saves than guys like John Hiller and Willie Hernandez, who preceded him. Todd was a very skilled relief pitcher who ended up with a good career and impressive numbers. I tip my hat to him. I just believe Hiller and Hernandez were a little bit better.

You might say that the change in the way relief pitchers, or closers, were used started with **Mike Henneman**, at least so far as the Tigers are concerned. Henneman, who preceded Todd Jones as the Tigers' closer, was groomed for that job in the minor leagues and was the first Tigers reliever to never start a major league game.

In 1983, Henneman was drafted by Toronto but didn't sign. That same year, he was drafted by the Phillies but didn't sign. In 1984, he was drafted by the Tigers and did sign. He spent four seasons in the minor leagues and appeared in 117 games but made only one start.

Mike got to the Tigers in 1987, the year I left, so I just missed catching him. I did hit against him later when I returned to the American League, and I can attest personally to his ability. I faced him eight times and had one hit off him, a single.

In his rookie season, the Tigers' system was closer-by-committee. Mike shared the job with Eric King and Willie Hernandez and saved seven games. It was a sign of the times that he also won 11 games and averaged 1.74 innings per outing.

In 1988, Sparky Anderson made Henneman the Tigers' No. 1 closer. Over the next six seasons, Henneman saved 121 games and had at least 21 saves in five of the six years but never more than 24 in any one season.

Mike Henneman was the first pitcher groomed by the Tigers exclusively as a closer, and when he retired, he was the team's leader in saves.

Henneman was traded to Houston late in the 1995 season. When he left Detroit, he was the Tigers' all-time saves leader with 154 but has since been replaced in the top spot by Todd Jones.

Like John Hiller, Mike Henneman could have had many more saves if he had been used the way closers are used now.

"Señor Smoke!"

Aurelio Lopez was a piece of work. He was just magic in my eyes. I don't even know how he was as successful as he was. I can't tell you how many times he'd throw a fastball right down the middle of the plate and the hitter would swing right through it. It baffled me. *How'd he miss that?* It was like it was an optical illusion that made hitters miss.

Lopez also had a very good screwball. He was one of the first pitchers I caught who had a legitimate screwball. By that I mean a pitch thrown by a right-handed pitcher that you could clearly see break away from a left-handed

"Señor Smoke," as we called him, was a great screwball pitcher and a likable teammate.

hitter. I was impressed with that. I don't even know how a pitcher can get his arm in a position to get a ball to do that. I do know the screwball was a pitch that was popular in the 1930s and 1940s, but until Lopey came along I had never seen anybody throw it. It had to put a strain on a pitcher's elbow because he needs to twist his arm in a reverse motion from the curveball to throw it.

Lopey did a great job for us. Before Willie Hernandez got to Detroit and when John Hiller was at the end of his career, Señor Smoke was the man. He thrived on a lot of work and seemed to be better suited as a multiple-inning set-up man.

In 1979, he won 10 games, saved 21, and averaged more than two innings per outing. In 1980, he won 13 games, again saved 21, and averaged slightly less than two innings per outing. Over the next four seasons, he was used more and more in the set-up role. He won 27 games, saved 38, and averaged anywhere from 1.9 to 2.8 innings per outing.

Lopey was always entertaining to watch. I had my share of communication problems with him because we had a language barrier. Aurelio was from Mexico. I knew he understood what I was saying, but he would play dumb with me when it was convenient for him.

But I enjoyed being around him. He was a fun guy—always laughing, always smiling, just a big, jolly guy. I don't know how he kept himself in shape to pitch as often as he did, because he looked like he was going to blow out any minute. He would never have won any swimsuit competitions, but whenever he had to, he always answered the manager's call.

Lopey put Tabasco sauce on everything he ate and in everything he drank. He carried a large bottle of it in his bag. We'd get on an airplane and I would sit next to him sometimes and the stewardess would bring drinks and Lopey would take out his bottle of Tabasco sauce, shake it a few times, and pour it in his drink.

He also loved chili peppers. The hotter they were, the better he liked them. He'd often carry around a jar of them, and he would pluck a couple of peppers out of the jar and munch them down. I once saw him pull out the last pepper in a jar, chomp it down, and then drink the juice that remained in the jar.

"Lopey," I said. "How could you drink that? You must have a cast-iron stomach. Nobody can eat and drink what you do and survive."

He just started laughing.

I enjoyed Lopez a lot, and I was saddened when I heard about his tragic end. He was killed in an automobile accident in his native Mexico the day after his 44th birthday.

Statistical Summaries

All statistics are for player's Tigers career only.

PITCHING

G = Games
W = Games won
L = Games lost
PCT = Winning percentage
SV = Saves
SO = Strikeouts
ERA = Earned-run average

Relief Pitcher	Years	G	W	L	PCT	SV	SO	ERA
John Hiller *Struck out seven consecutive Cleveland batters on 10/1/70*	1965–70, 1972–80	545	87	76	.534	125	1,036	2.83
Willie Hernandez *Didn't blow a save opportunity until final weekend of 1984 MVP season*	1984–89	358	36	31	.537	120	384	2.98

continued	Years	G	W	L	PCT	SV	SO	ERA
Todd Jones *Had four saves and 0.00 ERA in seven postseason appearances in 2006*	1997–2001, 06–08	480	23	32	.418	235	372	4.07
Mike Henneman *Posted 10 or more wins in consecutive odd-numbered seasons (1987, 1989, and 1991)*	1987–95	491	57	34	.626	154	480	3.05
Aurelio Lopez *Credited with a victory in both the ALCS and World Series in 1984*	1979–85	355	53	30	.639	85	519	3.41

FIELDING

PO = Putouts

A = Assists

E = Errors

DP = Double plays

TC/G = Total chances divided by games played

FA = Fielding average

Relief Pitcher	PO	A	E	DP	TC/G	FA
John Hiller	45	136	8	5	0.3	.958
Willie Hernandez	25	57	2	4	0.2	.976
Todd Jones	24	49	3	3	0.2	.961
Mike Henneman	53	76	8	8	0.3	.942
Aurelio Lopez	35	75	6	6	0.3	.948

TWELVE

Manager

I'll be very candid about this. I wasn't exactly doing cartwheels or jumping for joy when the Tigers announced they had hired **Sparky Anderson** to be their manager.

Nothing against Sparky. I didn't know him, had never met him, and don't remember ever having any previous contact with him, good or bad. I certainly knew who he was and what he had accomplished: manager of the Cincinnati Reds' "Big Red Machine," four National League pennants, two World Series championships, and a winning percentage of almost .600 in nine years. How could you not be impressed with a résumé like that?

My reasons for not being thrilled when Sparky came aboard were purely selfish. I was 23 years old and I had just begun playing regularly for the Tigers.

1.	SPARKY ANDERSON
2.	MICKEY COCHRANE
3.	MAYO SMITH
4.	STEVE O'NEILL
5.	HUGHIE JENNINGS

When I came up for 12 games in 1977 and then when I was up to stay in 1978, my manager was Ralph Houk, who was a players' manager. He also was a former catcher, and I learned a lot from him. When I caught 79 games in 1978, I figured Houk was grooming me to take over as the regular catcher.

Then all of a sudden Houk was gone. He left the Tigers to manage the Red Sox. I was sorry to see Houk go, but when the Tigers named Les Moss as Houk's replacement, I was elated. Not only was Les another former catcher, he had been my manager at Double A Montgomery and Triple A Evansville—and he was near and dear to my heart. I honestly believe that if it wasn't for Les Moss, I might not have made it to the big leagues. He was that instrumental in my development as a player in the minor leagues.

Moss might not have been the communicator the Tigers were looking for in a major league manager or the big name that Sparky Anderson was, but I thought he was an extremely good manager. And because I had a history with him, I was upbeat about playing for him again. We started the 1979 season slowly but had a good West Coast trip and climbed over .500 with a record of 27–26. Of our 53 games, I had started 48, so I was feeling pretty good about my situation. Then came the shocker. Moss was out and Sparky Anderson—who had been let go by the Reds the previous year after nine seasons—was coming in to take over as manager.

It was no knock on Les, but when you get a chance to hire a manager with Anderson's name, his résumé, and his experience, you try to get him if you can. That was apparently what the Tigers were thinking. It wasn't what I was thinking.

Here was someone who had managed probably the greatest catcher in the history of the game, Johnny Bench, about whom Sparky once said, "Don't embarrass any catcher by comparing him to Johnny Bench."

Would Sparky be too demanding of any other catcher? Would he look to replace me with another catcher more to his liking, a veteran perhaps?

I was a bit uneasy, to say the least, when Sparky took over. When he came in, there was immediately a completely different atmosphere in our clubhouse. Here was a guy who had been very successful in Cincinnati, who was very well known, highly esteemed, and respected. It was like bringing in a rock star.

It was obvious from the beginning that Sparky came with a game plan, because he started making changes right away. Whether it was Sparky's idea or whether it came from Jim Campbell, the Tigers' president and general manager, and Bill Lajoie, the director of player development, I don't know. What I do know is that players were being shuffled out. When Sparky came into town, the older players started leaving town.

Sparky Anderson's success as a manager speaks for itself. I am glad to have played during his tenure.

Fortunately, even before Sparky got there, the Tigers had begun a youth movement. Sparky inherited a team that included Lou Whitaker, Alan Trammell, Jason Thompson, Steve Kemp, Jack Morris, Dan Petry, Kirk Gibson, and me, not one of us older than 24. That's a pretty good nucleus on which to build, and it turned out that Sparky was the right guy to be in charge of the construction.

We soon found out that Sparky had his way of doing things and he was adamant about them. In Cincinnati, he had a dress code and a no-facial-hair rule, and he brought those rules with him to Detroit.

Aurelio Rodriguez, our third baseman, had a big, beautiful mustache. When Sparky told him he had to get rid of it, I thought "Chi-Chi" was going to cry. That mustache was his trademark look, and then Sparky Anderson rolled in and it was, "New sheriff in town, boys, and these are the rules."

After a short period of time, Sparky relented. He allowed mustaches, but that was it—no beards, no mutton chops, and no jeans on the road. You had to be well groomed. Sparky was a stickler on appearance, and he demanded that his players look and act professionally. We had to wear jackets and ties on airplanes. To this day, I respect that. I see how a lot of professional athletes dress these days, and I think it's a shame. As major leaguers, they are setting an example—or they should be. They are representing not only their team, but also the city in which they play, and I believe they should dress and act accordingly.

In the beginning, it was difficult making the adjustment to Sparky's way of doing things. He was a disciplinarian. He made it clear that it was his way or the highway. He had the authority in those days that, if he didn't like you or you didn't measure up to his laws and expectations, you were history. He made no bones about telling players, "You either do things the way I tell you to do them or you won't be around here. It's as simple as that." We saw that demonstrated on more that one occasion. We knew he had the power; if he wanted you gone, you were gone.

He insisted that his players respect everybody in the clubhouse, and that included the guy who ran the clubhouse, the kids who worked for the club-house man, the equipment manager, the batboys…everybody who walked through those doors.

He expected that players treated the media with respect and answered their questions. "They have a job to do, too," he said. "You have to appreciate that. It's not fair for them to come in here and for you guys to ignore them or be rude to them or insult them or try to avoid them."

Sparky had a way of coming up with analogies to make his point. For example, he might say, "At home I have a garden. When I'm at home in the off-season, I like to tend to my garden. I grow my flowers and I grow my vegetables and I take very good care of them, but every once in awhile a weed will pop up. That weed disturbs my whole program with my garden, so whenever I see a weed pop up—just like on this team, when somebody goes against the grain or is not with the program— I'd pluck that weed right out of my garden and it would be gone."

We got the message. When he wanted something done, you just did it. You never questioned his reason.

When Kirk Gibson first came up, he was extremely competitive and headstrong. He wanted to be in the lineup all the time. On more than one occasion, Gibby and Sparky clashed over playing time. Gibson wanted to be in the lineup every day, but Sparky didn't want him playing against certain pitchers and used him in a platoon situation for a while. Gibson thought he was right; Sparky *knew* he was right. So Sparky said, "You know what? We're going to do something here, and you're going to realize who's running this show and that I'll tell you when you're going to play. From now on, I'm going to have you sit on the bench right next to me during games until you figure out who the manager of this team is."

Gibson was pulled out of the lineup, and Sparky didn't play him until Gibby broke. Eventually, Anderson came to appreciate and respect Gibby's desire and determination, and Gibson came to respect Sparky's discipline and knowledge of the game.

I had my own little run-ins with Sparky. Early on in his tenure, I was called into his office. He said that Roger Craig, our pitching coach, was going to call all the pitches from the dugout. I didn't know how to take that. Were they insinuating that I was doing a bad job or that I was calling a bad game? They never explained their reasoning, but I had to look to myself as at least part of the problem.

Then there was an article in *Sports Illustrated* that quoted Sparky saying, "Either we have the dumbest pitchers in the major leagues or something else is the problem."

Well, the only other "something else" there could be was me, so I went in to Sparky and we went at it. He said, "Nah, that's not what I meant." We went toe-to-toe on that issue, but we straightened it out and we went on to have a good relationship. Sparky never said anything like his remark about not embarrassing anybody by comparing him to Johnny Bench, and I never took offense with that because he never made that an issue. All I took that comment to mean was that he had a tremendous amount of respect for Johnny Bench—so do I. And so does everybody else.

There were times when I was summoned into Sparky's office to discuss something and he'd sit me down and start talking, and I'd be in there for a half hour until he'd say, "Okay, get out of here." I'd walk out and think, *I have no idea what he just said for the last half hour.* He went from one subject to the next, to the next and I always came out feeling the same way.

I came to enjoy being around Sparky. He would double-talk and speak ungrammatically, but I knew Sparky well enough to know that he was dumb like a fox. Whatever he did, whatever he said, and the way he said it, it was all for a reason. If he was double-talking, he was making a subtle point. And he is smart enough to know the difference between good grammar and bad. He obviously had a method to his madness.

The bottom line is his record. In the eight years I played for Sparky in Detroit, we never had a losing record, and we won the World Series in 1984. Sparky spent 26 years as a manager, the seventh-longest tenure in baseball history. His 2,194 wins are sixth best all-time. He was elected to the Hall of Fame in 2000.

After what was an uncertain start based on my apprehension and insecurity, I came to respect Sparky and enjoy playing for him. I learned from him, I believe I profited from playing for him, and I consider him a friend to this day. We stay in touch. I've played in his charity golf tournaments, he's played in mine, and we exchange Christmas cards each year.

I have nothing but the utmost respect for him. I would put his ability to manage a team up there with anybody. Don't judge him by his poor grammar—I believe it's just a ploy. It doesn't do justice to his intelligence as a man and as a manager, one of the game's great thinkers who, in my opinion, could outstrategize anybody.

Just about every baseball fan is familiar with **Mickey Cochrane**, whose lifetime batting average of .320 is the highest of any catcher in history and who was the third catcher elected to the Hall of Fame. Not so many fans, however, remember his managing career.

In 1933, Cochrane was still in the prime of his career, playing for the Philadelphia Athletics, when A's owner/manager Connie Mack, strapped for cash, began dismantling his team and conducted a sale of some of his more valuable assets. Lefty Grove, Rube Walberg, and Max Bishop went to the Red Sox for $125,000 and two players, and the Tigers, looking to upgrade at the catcher position, sent Mack another $100,000 for Cochrane.

The Tigers, at the time, were leaderless, Bucky Harris having resigned as manager after a five-year run in which he failed to finish out of the second division. Tigers owner Frank Navin had offered the job to the one and only Babe Ruth. But he who hesitates, and when Ruth procrastinated and asked Navin to hold off until Babe returned from a series of personal appearances in Hawaii, the Tigers' owner, eager for a quick resolution to his managerial

Better known as a player than a manager, Mickey Cochrane (far left) was signed as both when he came over from Philadelphia. Also pictured are (left to right) Cincinnati manager Bill McKechnie, an unidentified umpire, umpire George Magerkurth, and Tigers catcher Rudy York.

problem, made a daring and surprising decision. He named Cochrane the team's player/manager.

Although he had never managed before, Cochrane had earned a reputation as a leader, an intelligent player, and a fierce competitor dating back to his undergraduate days at Boston University, where he played five sports. In football, Cochrane was BU's quarterback, leading running back, punter, and occasional part-time trainer and coach on the field.

With the Athletics, his temper and fiery competitiveness earned him the name "Black Mike." Said teammate Doc Cramer, "Lose a 1–0 game and you didn't want to get into the clubhouse with Grove and Cochrane. You'd be ducking stools and gloves and bats and whatever else would fly."

In his first season as manager, Cochrane improved the Tigers by 26 games and moved them up from fifth place to first, capturing the team's first pennant in 25 years. The following season, they finished first again and beat the Cubs in six games to win the first World Series in Detroit history. It was Cochrane who scored the winning run in the bottom of the ninth in the clinching Game 6. He later called it "My greatest day in baseball."

Six weeks after the Tigers' greatest triumph, owner Frank Navin suffered a heart attack and died. Walter Briggs, who owned 50 percent of the team's stock, bought Navin's share and took over running the team. One of his first moves was to make Cochrane vice president and general manager in addition to field manager. The dual role proved to be too much for Cochrane. He seemed to cave under the pressure and suffered a breakdown. After 120 games, Briggs sent Cochrane home and replaced him with Del Baker, who brought the Tigers home in second place.

Cochrane returned in 1937, but on May 25 in Yankee Stadium, he was hit on the head by a pitch from the Yankees' Bump Hadley and sustained a triple skull fracture. For several days, Cochrane hovered between life and death. He would never play again, but he recovered enough to resume managing and, for the second straight season, the Tigers finished in second place.

By 1938, Cochrane's ability to serve as both manager and general manager was in serious question. The beaning seemed to have stripped him of his competitive desire. On August 6, with the Tigers floundering with a record of 47–51, Del Baker again replaced him.

Cochrane would remain in baseball with several teams as a coach, scout, and general manager, but he would never manage again. His record as a manager was 348–250, and he had a winning percentage of .582, which is the highest for a Tigers manager with at least one full year of service.

The third time was the charm for **Mayo Smith**. In his first two tries as a manager in the major leagues, in Philadelphia and Cincinnati, he took over a team either too late (Philadelphia) or too early (Cincinnati) and bombed out. But he rang the bell on his third try, in Detroit.

A career minor leaguer who spent almost 20 seasons in the bushes, Smith made it to the big leagues for 73 games with the Philadelphia Athletics in 1945 and batted a tepid .212. When his playing career ended, Smith became a

Time was on Mayo Smith's side. In his second year as manager, the Tigers won a World Series championship.

minor league manager in the Yankees' farm system and got his first chance to manage in the major leagues with the Phillies in 1955.

Only a few years earlier, the Phillies' "Whiz Kids" were the talk of baseball. But the Whiz Kids were aging when Smith arrived, and they finished fourth, fifth, and fifth, respectively, in his first three years. When the Phillies got off to a 39–45 start in 1958, Smith was let go as manager and replaced by Eddie Sawyer.

Less than a year later, Smith got his second chance when he was named manager of the Cincinnati Reds to start the 1959 season. This time he got off to a 35–45 start, not making it past the All-Star Game before he was fired. Two seasons later, led by Frank Robinson and Vada Pinson, the Reds won the National League pennant.

Smith returned to the Yankees as a superscout. In 1967 the Tigers came calling, and Smith got his third chance. This time the timing was right. To a corps of veterans—Al Kaline, Norm Cash, Jim Northrup, Earl Wilson, and Hank Aguirre—the Tigers had added such promising newcomers as Bill Freehan, Willie Horton, Mickey Stanley, and a couple of pitchers named Denny McLain and Mickey Lolich.

The Tigers won 91 games but lost the second game of a doubleheader to the California Angels on the final day of the season and finished a game behind the Red Sox. The following season, however, the Tigers won 103 games and with McLain winning 31, finished 12 games ahead of the Orioles to win the American League pennant.

The Tigers would face the heavily favored St. Louis Cardinals in the World Series, and Smith would face a dilemma. He had skillfully rotated four out-fielders during the season, veterans Northrup and Kaline—the latter winding down his Hall of Fame career—and youngsters Horton and Stanley. Their bats had combined for 78 home runs and 288 RBI and were an important part of the team's offense.

With the designated hitter still five years in the future, Smith pondered how to get the most production from his four outfielders. His solution was a bold and controversial one. He opted for offense over defense. He had planned ahead during the season by having his center fielder, Stanley, play nine games at shortstop, and he announced that Stanley would be his short-stop in the World Series in place of the feeble-hitting Ray Oyler, who had batted an anemic .135 with one home run and 12 RBI in 215 at bats.

Northrup moved from right field to center to replace Stanley and was flanked by Kaline in right and Horton in left. The gamble paid off big time for Smith, even though Stanley struggled at bat and hit only .214. But Northrup, Kaline, and Horton combined for five home runs and 19 RBI, and the Tigers won the World Series, due mainly to the pitching of Mickey Lolich, who beat the Cardinals three times, including a 4–1, complete game, five-hit victory over Bob Gibson in Game 7 on only two days' rest.

The second youngest and most successful of four brothers that played in the major leagues, **Steve O'Neill** was a catcher for 17 seasons with the Indians, Red Sox, Yankees, and St. Louis Browns. But he is best known as a manage-rial Mr. Fix-It, a part of the old boys' network of managers in the '30s, '40s, and '50s. He also was Mr. Available, Mr. Dependable, and Mr. Experience among managers.

A journeyman as a player, Steve O'Neill was also a manager of four major league teams during his long baseball career.

Need a quick fix for your struggling team? Call Steve O'Neill.

Looking for a calm, steady, experienced hand to guide an out-of-control roster of malcontents and cut-ups? O'Neill is your man.

O'Neill managed four teams: the Indians, Tigers, Red Sox, and Phillies. With the Indians, Red Sox, and Phillies, he was hired midseason. Each time he took over a team, during or at the start of a season, he delivered immediate improvement.

In 14 seasons or parts thereof, O'Neill never posted a losing record, finishing with a total mark of 1,040 wins and 821 losses and a winning percentage of .559 which is a higher percentage than Walter Alston, Bobby Cox, Billy Martin, Sparky Anderson, Hughie Jennings, Joe Torre, Tony La Russa, Whitey Herzog, Tommy Lasorda, Lou Piniella, Dick Williams, Terry Francona, Connie Mack, and Casey Stengel.

In 1943, O'Neill was named manager of the Tigers, replacing Del Baker. He improved the Tigers by five games, winning 78. In 1944 he led the Tigers to 88 wins and a second-place finish. He followed that with 88 wins in 1945—not to mention the Tigers' seventh pennant and second World Series title. In the next two years he won 92 and 85 games, finishing second both times. When he fell off to 78 wins and fifth place in 1948, Red Rolfe replaced him. O'Neill finished 509–414 with the Tigers and a winning percentage of .551.

There was no Manager of the Year Award presented by baseball in the first two decades of the 20th century. If there had been, **Hughie Jennings** might have won it a few times.

If not baseball's Manager of the Year award, Jennings certainly would have qualified as a candidate for the Nobel Peace Prize given the way he galvanized the Tigers and managed to keep his players from killing their star center fielder, Ty Cobb, and vice versa. It was Jennings' ability to cope with his star's eccentricities and "let Cobb be Cobb" that contributed to his success as a manager.

One of Jennings' first moves when he took over as manager of the Tigers in 1907 was to switch Cobb from center field to right to separate him from left fielder Marty McIntyre, with whom Cobb openly feuded. Under Jennings, Cobb blossomed as a megastar for the Tigers. In his third major league season, he batted .350 to win the first of his 11 American League batting titles and drove in 119 runs to win the first of his four RBI crowns.

One of Detroit's most colorful characters, Hughie Jennings does his trademark "Ee-Yah" dance.

And the Tigers, who had won only 71 games and finished sixth the previous year, won 92 games and the first of three straight pennants under Jennings.

Jennings came out of the Pennsylvania coal mines to become one of the finest baseball players of his day, a brilliant fielding shortstop and a dangerous and reliable hitter. He cut his baseball eyeteeth with the famed Baltimore Orioles of John McGraw, Wilbert Robinson, Wee Willie Keeler, and Ned Hanlon. It was there he adopted the rambunctious, aggressive, and fiery style that would remain his trademark throughout his baseball career as player (in seven years with the Orioles, he was hit by pitches 205 times), coach, and manager.

Jennings would become one of baseball's best loved and most colorful characters in his time, a man who once suffered a fractured skull when he dove into an empty swimming pool and who attended law school in the off-season, passed the Maryland Bar Exam in 1905, and ran a thriving law practice between baseball seasons.

As a manager, Jennings became famous for his antics in the third-base coaching box, including whistles, horns, grass-plucking, gyrations, and his trademark, the "Ee-Yah" whoop that was accompanied by him waving his arms over his head and kicking up his right knee. Before long, he became known as Hughie "Ee-Yah" Jennings, and the sight of him appearing on the field would bring shouts of "Ee-Yah" from Tigers fans.

Jennings remained manager of the Tigers for 14 years but never won another pennant after his first three. Nevertheless, he remains one of the legendary heroes of Detroit Tigers baseball.

Statistical Summaries

All statistics are for manager's Tigers career only.

MANAGING

G = Games managed

W = Games won

L = Games lost

PCT = Winning percentage

P = Pennants

WS = World Series victories

Manager	Years	G	W	L	PCT	P	WS
Sparky Anderson *Managed four Championship Series sweeps (1970, '75, '76, '84)*	1979–95	2,580	1,331	1,248	.516	1	1
Mickey Cochrane *Player/manager in two of the five World Series he appeared in*	1934–38	600	348	250	.582	2	1

continued	Years	G	W	L	PCT	P	WS
Mayo Smith *Won 90 or more games each season from 1967–69*	1967–70	651	363	285	.560	1	1
Steve O'Neill *Finished first or second each year from 1944–47*	1943–48	933	509	414	.551	1	1
Hughie Jennings *Won pennants each of his first three seasons as manager (1907–09)*	1907–20	2,127	1,131	972	.538	3	0

Epilogue

He never threw a pitch for the Tigers, never got a hit, never scored a run. He never wore the Tigers uniform, never got his name in a box score. And yet, he is as much a part of Detroit Tigers baseball as Ty Cobb, Charlie Gehringer, and Mickey Cochrane, his name as familiar to Tigers fans as Hank Greenberg, Al Kaline, and Hal Newhouser.

For almost a half century, Ernie Harwell was "the Voice of the Tigers," his syrupy sweet Georgia accent so much a part of the lives of fans throughout the state of Michigan and beyond.

To those who have been associated with the Tigers for any part of that half-century, Ernie Harwell is not just a voice. There is a man behind that voice—a gentle, kind, compassionate man who was always there with a kind word, to help, counsel, and support—a man whose inclination was to encourage, not disparage, to praise, not condemn.

Ernie was born in Washington, Georgia, on January 15, 1918. You do the math. His centennial is not far off, and yet he remains a vibrant, energetic, enthusiastic Tiger to this day. His love affair with the game of baseball dates to his childhood when he began, at the age of five, serving as the visiting batboy for the Atlanta Crackers of the Southern Association.

After graduating from Emory University, Ernie began a career as a sportswriter for the Atlanta *Constitution,* which ultimately led to a gig as an announcer of Crackers games. A four-year hitch in the U.S. Marines during World War II interrupted and stalled Ernie's broadcasting career, but he returned after the war to resume broadcasting Crackers games. In 1948,

Ernie Harwell

fate—and Branch Rickey—intervened, and Ernie became the only announcer in baseball history to be traded for a player.

With the Brooklyn Dodgers' announcer, Red Barber, (like Harwell, a Southern voice) hospitalized with a bleeding ulcer, Rickey needed a substitute and decided Harwell was his man. But the Crackers were reluctant to part with their popular "voice" unless they were compensated. Rickey agreed to send catcher Cliff Dapper to Atlanta in exchange for Harwell's tonsils.

Harwell spent the next 12 years moving from the Dodgers to the New York Giants to the Baltimore Orioles, always as a backup announcer. His big break came in 1960 when the Tigers were seeking a lead announcer to replace the popular Van Patrick. Ernie was their choice.

Harwell arrived in Detroit in 1960 to broadcast the games of a team that would finish in sixth place in the American League with a record of 71–83 under three managers—Jimmie Dykes, Billy Hitchcock, and Joe Gordon—

and despite the presence of such Tigers luminaries as Norm Cash, Charlie Maxwell, Rocky Colavito, Jim Bunning, Frank Lary, and a 25-year-old right fielder in his eighth major league season by the name of Al Kaline.

Ernie became known not only for his smooth, low-key delivery but also for his down-home humor and his trademark phrases such as "He took his cut and now he takes his seat" when describing a swinging strikeout, and "That ball is looooong gone," when describing a home run.

With the exception of 1992, when he worked a part-time schedule for the California Angels after his Tigers contract was not renewed by the Tigers and the team's radio station, Harwell spent 42 years as the Tigers' announcer, retiring after the 2002 season, He still returns to Comerica Park on occasion to serve as a guest commentator.

Along the way, Harwell has made enormous contributions to the game of baseball apart from his broadcasting. He has written essays and poems about the game he loves and has written many songs, 66 of which have been recorded by such artists as Homer and Jethro. Ernie received the ultimate honor for his profession in 1981 when he became the fifth broadcaster to receive the National Baseball Hall of Fame's prestigious Ford C. Frick Award.

I cherish a lot of great memories. I have met a lot of great people, and have made many good friends in my years as a player, coach, and television broadcaster with the Tigers. On the top of that list is getting to know Ernie Harwell and having the privilege of calling him my friend.

Index

Sunday games, 88–89
Swift, Bob, 116
switch-hitters, Tigers, 11, 57

Tanana, Frank, 162–64, 169
Templeton, Garry, 49
Tettleton, Mickey, 7, 8, 9, 11–12, 16, 64
Texas League, 26, 148
Texas Rangers, 1, 74, 75, 106
Thames, Marcus, 53
third basemen, Tigers, 63–77
Thomas, Gorman, 55
Thompson, Jason, 187
three generations of major league ballplayers,
    66–69
Tiger of the Year award, 60
Tiger Stadium, Detroit, 17, 24, 26, 30, 38, 57,
    70, 121, 147–48
Tigertown, Lakeland, Florida, 106, 111, 158
Tinker, Joe, 40
Toronto Blue Jays, 28
Torre, Joe, 196
Tracewski, Dick, 44
trades, baseball
    announcer traded for player, 202
    Boone in eight-player trade, 67
    Cash trade, 25
    Evers in nine-player trade, 111
    Guillen–Santiago trade, 55
    Hernandez trade, 176
    Jones in nine-player trade, 177
    Kemp-Lemon trade, 103–4
    Kuenn-Colavito trade, 53–54, 84–85
    Manush trade, 90, 92
    Miguel Cabrera, 32
    Owen trade, 71
    Polanco trade, 43
Trammell, Alan, 49–53, 61, 62
    as manager, 42, 101, 130
    Whitaker and, 38, 40, 64, 73, 105, 111, 187
Triandos, Gus, 9
triples record, major league career, 125
Trout, Dizzy, 151
Trucks, Virgil "Fire," 151

University of Arizona, 30
University of Illinois at Urbana-Champaign,
    109

University of Michigan, 2, 35, 69
University of Southern California, 126
University of Tennessee, 143
University of Wisconsin–Madison, 53
Upshaw, Willie, 28
Urbina, Ugueth, 43
Utley, Chase, 43

Veach, Bobby, 35–36, 79–81, 90, 93, 94, 121
Verlander, Justin, 151

Wagner, Honus, 40, 95, 121
Walberg, Rube, 190
walks, in the American League, 12
Washington Senators, 59, 81, 86, 87, 90, 92,
    137, 144
Weaver, Earl, 146, 176–77
Webb, Skeeter, 46
Werber, Billy, 72
Whitaker, Lou, 38–41, 47, 48, 64, 73, 105, 111,
    187
White, Frank, 40
Williams, Dick, 196
Williams, Ted, 26, 28, 59, 65–66, 69, 88, 119,
    157, 165
Wilson, Earl, 151, 194
Wilson, Glenn, 176
Wilson, Willie, 128
Wockenfuss, John, 176
World Series
    1934, Tigers vs. Cardinals, 58, 70–71, 87,
        143, 149
    1935, Tigers vs. Cubs, 20, 71, 90, 143–44,
        149, 192
    1945, Tigers vs. Cubs, 46, 73
    1968, Tigers vs. Cardinals, 3, 26, 44–45, 81,
        83, 158, 159, 160, 194
    1984, Tigers vs. Padres, 39–40, 50, 104, 139,
        175
    1988, Dodgers vs. Oakland A's, 129–30
World War II, players in military service
    during, 18, 21, 28, 45, 109, 201

Yankee Stadium, Bronx, New York, 19, 29, 66,
    90, 166, 192
York, Rudy, 21, 26–28, 33, 34, 191
Young, Cy, 79
Yount, Robin, 49, 55